Baseline Assessment and Monitoring in Primary Schools

Achievements, Attitudes and Value-added Indicators

Peter Tymms

David Fulton Publishers

London

David Fulton Publishers Ltd
Ormond House, 26–27 Boswell Street, London WC1N 3JZ
www.fultonpublishers.co.uk

First published in Great Britain by David Fulton Publishers 1999
Reprinted 2000

Note: The right of Peter Tymms to be identified as the authors of this work has been asserted by him in accordance with the Copyright, Designs and Patents Act 1988.

British Library Cataloguing in Publication Data
A catalogue record for this book is available from the British Library

ISBN 1–85346–591–7

Typeset by Kate Williams, Abergavenny
Printed in Great Britain by Bell & Bain Ltd, Glasgow

Contents

Preface

Education is top of the agenda. Politicians have said so and they know, they take notice of their focus groups and surveys. This recognition, in England, has resulted in a staggering series of measures designed to improve the system. In the last decade we have seen the introduction of a National Curriculum, systematic testing from the ages of 4 to 18, league tables, OFSTED, the identification of failing schools, the literacy and numeracy hours, Beacon Schools and Education Action Zones. The list is endless and the effort of those caught up in it all is enormous. Within the turmoil it is easy to lose sight of the bigger picture and this short book is designed to give an objective overview of the achievements, progress and attitudes of pupils in their primary schools. It does this by drawing on one of the most successful projects run within schools. The project, Performance Indicators in Primary Schools (PIPS), is designed to monitor schools for the benefit of schools.

The book takes a scientific approach to research and seeks always to give a view that is backed by good quality data. The intention is nevertheless to be accessible and, to that end, detailed references are not given in the main body of the text but are kept to the summaries at the end of each chapter. For the sake of accessibility the text is written in the present tense. This can mislead. For example, when a survey shows that pupils in primary school like their schools it is proper to say that the pupils 'liked' their school. That is what was found. It is incorrect to assert that they are liking it now (present tense) and this phraseology will become increasingly inappropriate as the book dates. However, it makes for easier reading and it is hoped that the reader will forgive this lack of precision.

The last part of the book describes a view of education and research that may be unexpected to many readers. It emphasises our lack of knowledge and our uncertainty. It underlines the need for monitoring, and interventions, as well as raising the possibility of simulations. But while this perspective is uncommon among British educationalists the writer feels it to be important and earnestly hopes to persuade readers of the need for this kind of approach.

Acknowledgements

This book has grown out of work carried out at the Curriculum, Evaluation and Management (CEM) Centre, which probably runs the largest quantitative monitoring programme in the world. More specifically it reflects work around the Performance Indicators in Primary Schools (PIPS) project, the idea for which came from Professor Carol Fitz-Gibbon and it was she who organised the finances that helped to set up the project in 1993. Professor Fitz-Gibbon was responsible not only for this initial work but for the first monitoring project of the CEM Centre (the A Level Information System, ALIS) which has provided a model from which PIPS has drawn its strength.

The PIPS project owes much of its success to a hard-working team. Research Associate Simon Gallacher and secretary Hazel Glass were among the first people to work with me on the project during the CEM Centre's years at the University of Newcastle. The team has now expanded to nine members of staff at Durham, whose work on the project has been invaluable in the past years and without whom this book could not have been written. The Research Associates were Christine Merrell, Brian Henderson, John Fraser, Stephen Albone and Paul Jones; the Project Co-ordinator was Katharine Bailey; the Project Secretaries, Rohini Maini, Vicky Howard and Amanda Carr and the Projects Manager, Mark Wightman. The data entry service provided by Carol Hellier and her team has also been vital.

The initial development work for PIPS was carried out in volunteer schools in the Newcastle area and later in Solihull, Bradford, the Isle of Man, and several clusters of schools sponsored by the NAHT. I owe thanks to the teachers, heads, LEA staff and the NAHT for their invaluable assistance, advice and support.

Only space, not preference, prevents me from mentioning more people who have been so important to the development of the project, but I would like to express particular thanks to the following for their commitment to our work: David Moseley, Rod Bramald, Sue McKeown and Barbara Cottam.

I am also indebted to the patience of Beena, Vijay and Santosh in their assistance with the script.

To my mother and father

Chapter 1

Introduction

How do we know what we know about primary pupils and the progress that they make? The answers to such an apparently simple question are quite diverse. Clearly everyone involved with education in the primary years has first-hand knowledge of pupils and the way that they develop. This is important information, but it is held in the minds of many thousands of individual professionals and cannot readily be accessed by others. One could try to distil and pass on this information. Processes such as mentoring and teacher training do this, at least in part. Such information is also passed on informally from one teacher to another and in its totality forms a rich vein of professional working knowledge.

Other information comes from more formal attempts to learn about pupils and they come under the heading of educational research. But this general heading has a variety of sub-headings. Research into education is unique in being conducted by specialists in a bewildering variety of academic disciplines. There are historians, scientists, mathematicians, philosophers, sociologists, psychologists and others. Each makes a contribution to educational research, bringing their own techniques (and baggage) to the process. This book attempts to provide a picture of pupils using an approach that is uniquely suitable to providing an overview of the progress that they make in primary schools. It draws strength from information collected from thousands of pupils as part of the PIPS project. This information is collected through surveys, assessments and tests involving pupils throughout the primary age range.

A lot of material is presented and much of it is numerical. It is described in the text but it is also presented in a variety of charts some types of which will be familiar to the reader whilst others may be new. The first chapter describes four different forms of presentation and the metric 'Effect Size' which is used throughout. The next chapter takes a careful look at assessments in general and at baseline assessment in particular. Chapter 3 considers the differences between pupils and the way in which they develop during the primary years. Chapter 4 explores the concept of Value-added and how the results of assessments can be used to look at the progress that pupils make. This is followed by a consideration of their attitudes, including self-concepts.

The last two chapters are devoted to considering how change can be handled within education and how research can be organised to help find things out and assist in the planning of policy.

1.1 Bar charts and histograms

One of the simplest ways to show information is to use a bar chart. It can show how many people belong to particular categories. By way of example we will look at the responses of Year 6 pupils to one of the questions asked about their feelings towards school in the PIPS project. The pupils were asked to say how much they agreed with the statement: *People are nice to me at school.* They chose their responses from five options: *False. Mostly false. Sometimes true/sometimes false. Mostly true. True.* The responses[1] from 1998 are shown in Figure 1.1, which compares the results of girls and boys.

The most common response from both girls and boys is to choose 'True' with over 40 per cent of both sexes opting for this reply. To see this is very gratifying and it is also nice to note that less than 10 per cent of boys and of girls choose the 'False' option. Overall, the girls are slightly more positive than the boys in their responses. About 5 per cent more girls than boys pick the most positive response and more boys than girls pick the negative responses.

Whilst bar charts are used to show categories, histograms can be used to show information that is continuous. Examples of continuous data include age, scores on an arithmetic assessment, salaries, attitudes and self-concept. Although the last chart showed one aspect of the feelings of pupils about school it was organised into categories

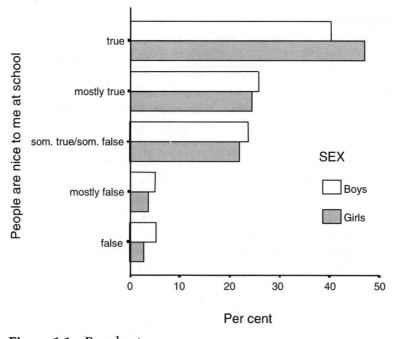

Figure 1.1   Bar chart

simply because that was how the information was collected. The pupils' feelings are not really in boxes, we created the categories artificially. Feelings are on a continuum. The example below shows a histogram of the scores of Year 6 pupils on a continuous measure called 'Attitude to School'. It was formed by averaging the pupils' responses to a series of statements about school. One of those items was discussed when looking at bar charts above and further examples follow:

- I look forward to school.
- I like my teachers.
- I like the lessons.

There were seven statements in all and for each one the pupils picked one of the five responses. These responses were given numbers from one to five with five being the most positive. The average response was then calculated to give an overall measure of Attitude to School. These responses are shown in the histogram in Figure 1.2.

The horizontal scale is given in numbers of pupils whereas in Figure 1.1 the horizontal scale is based on the percentage of pupils. It can be useful to see how many subjects are involved but proportions can also be informative and both are used in this book. The vertical scale runs from one to five and each bar represents the number of pupils within a particular range of scores from their responses to the seven questions. The distribution shows a marked tendency for pupils to pick the more positive responses. This tendency towards higher scores gives an asymmetrical spread of results that is known as a skewed distribution.

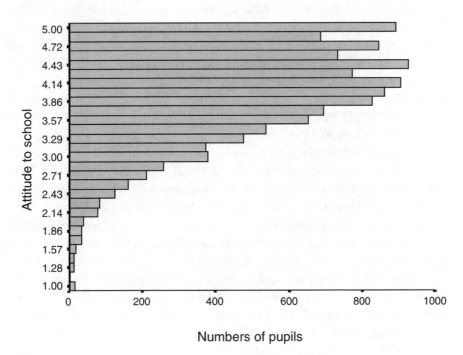

Figure 1.2 Histogram

1.2 Box-and-whisker plots

One nice way to summarise the kinds of data shown in the last diagram is to use box-and-whisker plots. They were invented by the statistician Tukey and are useful when dealing with continuous measures. Tukey's innovative diagrams are becoming quite common and are a useful way in which to look at information. They are used extensively in this book.

Box-and-whisker plots of the Attitude to School data, which was shown in the histogram earlier, are shown in Figure 1.3 for boys and girls separately.

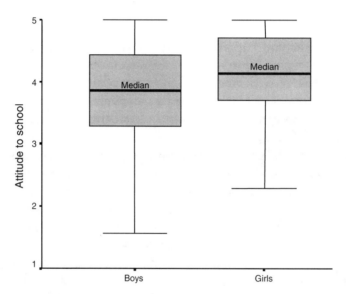

Figure 1.3   Box-and-whisker plots

The plots show how the Attitude to School scores are distributed. The two horizontal lines in the boxes show the middles of the two distributions. They are the medians and they divide the girls and boys into two equally sized groups. The two boxes each hold half of the boys and girls. A quarter of the boys and a quarter of the girls come above the boxes and a quarter below. The lowest lines of the boxes are the 25th percentiles – also know as the lower quartiles. The tops of the boxes are the 75th percentiles – also known as the upper quartiles. (A percentile indicates the percentage of pupils that obtain scores below the chosen one. The median, for example, is the 50th percentile since half of the pupils have scores below the median.)

The whiskers extend upwards to the highest score and downward to the lowest score. Unusual scores, known as outliers, may exist beyond the whiskers but for the sake of simplicity they are not shown in this book.

Figure 1.3 shows that scores are generally grouped towards the high end and the asymmetrical whiskers emphasise the skewness which is seen in Figure 1.2. The girls generally have higher scores on the Attitude to School scale than the boys. This is particularly noticeable at the more negative end of the scale where the boys dominate the chart. This is of educational significance. The chart shows that the majority of pupils at the top end of our primary schools and about to go to secondary school are very positive towards school. But there is a minority that do not like or enjoy school. Boys dominate this negative minority.

The average difference between girls and boys is clearly visible on the chart. The average score for boys was 3.81 and for girls it was 4.12. The next section shows how these averages can be presented together with estimates of how accurately they were measured. This is followed by a section that discusses how these averages can be used to find Effect Sizes – a crucial concept in educational research.

1.3 Confidence Intervals

We all know that measurements have uncertainties associated with them. Sometimes these uncertainties are regarded as so small that we tend not to be concerned with them in everyday life. However, even something as commonplace as measuring the length of an object with a ruler involves uncertainties. Indeed there are uncertainties with all measurements and it is important to recognise this whenever we use scores.

Assessments of knowledge and feelings are inherently less accurate than measures of length and it is particularly important to acknowledge the uncertainties surrounding those assessments. It is all too easy to assume that an assessment has pinned things down. To hear that Abigail has an IQ of 140 creates an inevitable impression but to know that the assessment had a stated uncertainty of plus or minus 20 puts a different complexion on the information.

The chart below (Figure 1.4) shows the average Attitude to School score for girls and boys together with the uncertainties surrounding those averages. The degrees of uncertainty, or certainty, are shown as the 95 per cent Confidence Intervals.

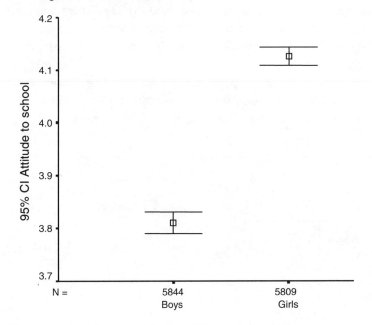

Figure 1.4 Means with Confidence Intervals

The little squares mark the average scores and the vertical bars above and below the squares mark the ends of the Confidence Intervals. The averages are estimates of the 'true' averages for Year 6 pupils but we cannot be sure that they are precise. We can, however, be fairly confident that the 'true' results lie somewhere within the horizontal lines which come at the ends at the vertical lines. Sometimes, but rarely, the 'true' result will be outside the vertical bars. In other words the Confidence Intervals are guides that help us gauge how accurately we have estimated the average for the boys and the girls. It is as though we look at measures through glasses that always make the results blurred and the confidence intervals give us a feel of how blurred the results are.

1.4 Effect Sizes

This book contains many comparisons. It compares girls with boys, twins with singles, schools with one another and so on. It compares them on attainment, developed ability and attitudes. This variety of presentations and measures presents a problem. All of the comparisons are unique and we might not be able to compare the comparisons! Are sex differences as important as age differences in a year group? Are schools most different in their pupils' developed ability or self-esteem? If we had one single way to answer the question 'How big was the difference?' we would be ideally placed. We would then be able to say whether sex differences for arithmetic were similar to sex differences for attitudes and so on. We would also be able to look at the relative importance of things like age, school attended and developed ability.

Fortunately there is a simple well-established way in which to compare groups on a universal metric. It involves the use of Effect Sizes, which in turn make use of the concept of Standard Deviation – a measure of the spread of scores. The Standard Deviation may be readily calculated using a computer or a calculator and its meaning may be understood mathematically through references that are given at the end of this chapter.

Here, a slightly different approach is taken. The concept is explained using words and diagrams. The Standard Deviation can be approached through the idea of deviations. A deviation is the differ-

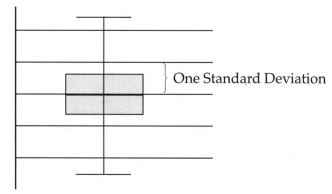

Figure 1.5   Box-and-whisker plot

ence between the average score and the score being considered. The Standard Deviation may be thought of as an average deviation, or the average distance from the mean.[2] This is not a precise definition mathematically but it should give an intuitive idea of its meaning. The Standard Deviation can be seen diagrammatically on the box-and-whisker plot, which is shown in Figure 1.5

About two thirds (68 per cent) of all pupils come within one Standard Deviation either side of the average. Almost all (95 per cent) come within two Standard Deviations and 99.9 per cent lie within three Standard Deviations.

Having tackled the idea of Standard Deviation we can now look at the meaning of Effect Size. It is often used to compare two groups and the Effect Size is the difference between the two groups expressed in Standard Deviation units. The three diagrams below (Figure 1.6a–c) show two groups that differ by increasing amounts. In the first diagram the two groups differ by 0.1 standard deviations, the second by 0.5 and the third by 0.8.

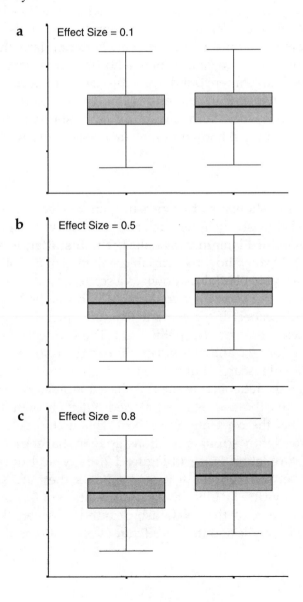

Figure 1.6

When we compared the Attitude to School of girls and boys we saw that they differed by 0.31 points (that is the difference between their average scores). This is almost a third of a mark on the five-point scale. Now we know that the Standard Deviation was 0.72 so the Effect Size is 0.31 divided by 0.72.[3] This gives an Effect Size of 0.43. In other words the girls were more positive towards school by about 0.4 Standard Deviations. This is a modest effect. Typically Effect Sizes around 0.2 are regarded as small, 0.5 is modest and 0.8 is thought of as being large.

A feel for Effect Sizes can be obtained by considering the things that men and women are most different at. Men tend to be better than women at throwing objects at targets (e.g. darts) and the Effect Size is about 0.8. Men also tend to be more restless than women with an Effect Size of 0.7. Women tend to be better at 'ideational fluency' (naming things) and the Effect Size is about 0.4. Women are also much better than men at 'reading' others' feelings with an Effect Size of 1.0.

When using Effect Sizes it is important to remember that they are summaries of group differences and that even with a large Effect Size there is still considerable overlap. Many individuals buck the trend. There are numerous women who are better at darts than the average man and there are many men who are more sensitive to others' feelings than women. But despite this caution Effect Sizes have many things in their favour and one of the big advantages of using Effect Sizes is that work from several different sources can be combined using a technique known as meta-analysis. More will be said of this later.

1.5 Scatterplots and correlations

Scatterplots show how two measures are related to one another. They are used extensively in research and form the basis of the explanation of Value-added later in this book. The four scatterplots in the Figures 1.7a to 1.7d show how two variables relate to one another. Figure 1.7d shows a scatterplot (also known as a scattergram) in which there is no correlation between the two variables. This is the kind of result that we would expect if we compared pupils' luck in a game of chance with their scores from a spelling test. The strongest correlation possible is 1 (or –1) and we never find such a strong relationship in educational research, but we do find high figures. For example, when checking the reliability of the PIPS baseline assessment we reassessed pupils after the teachers had carried out their own assessment and found that the correlation was 0.93. This is the test-retest reliability. This is a slightly stronger relationship than that shown in Figure 1.7a.

The correlation of 0.7 in Figure 1.7b is typical of the relationship found between pupils' test scores when they are separated by a couple of years. Finally the weak correlation of 0.3, in Figure 1.7c, is representative of the relationship found between the home background of pupils and their academic success at school.

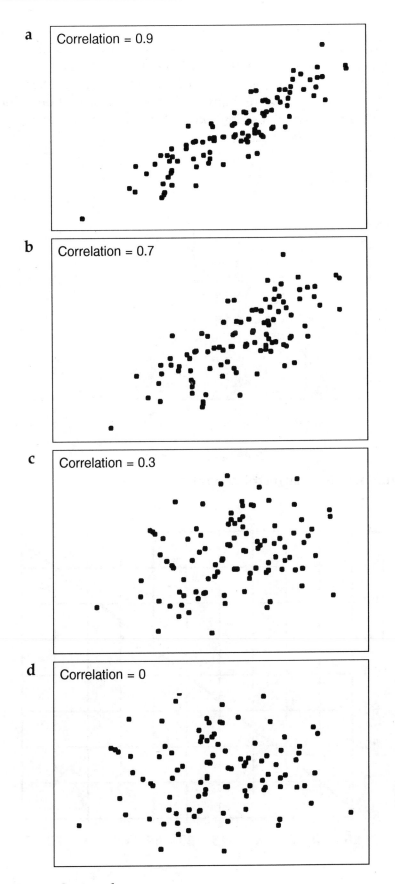

Figure 1.7 Scatterplot

1.6 Standardised scores

A standardised score is a score on a scale where the mean and Standard Deviation are fixed. In this book we have used a standardisation in which the mean is 50 and the Standard Deviation is 10. These scores are called 'T scores'. When reporting reading scores, for example, we will use a T score. Figure 1.8 shows a distribution, which is very close to a normal distribution, and in which the scores have been standardised to give T scores.

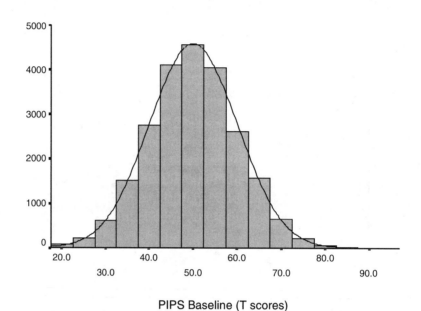

PIPS Baseline (T scores)

Figure 1.8   Normal distribution

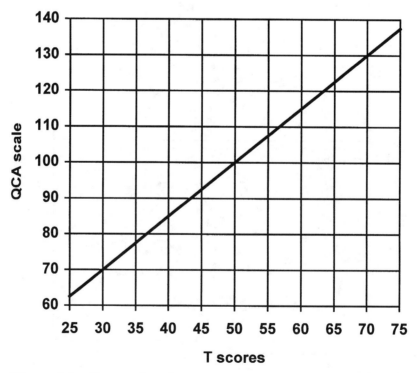

Figure 1.9   Conversion chart

Readers may be familiar with the scale used by the Qualifications and Curriculum Authority (QCA) for age corrected reading scores in which the mean is 100 and the Standard Deviation is 15. There are a number of other commonly used standard scores with different means and Standard Deviations but once the ideas behind them are clear there is no need to go any further. Some readers may want to convert T scores to QCA reading scores or vice versa and Figure 1.9 allows one to do that.

In a similar way, T scores can be related to percentiles and Figure 1.10 can be used to read off percentiles. As expected, a T score of 50 corresponds to the 50th percentile, which is also known as the median. A T score of 70 is close to the 97th percentile indicating that about 97 per cent get a score below 70.

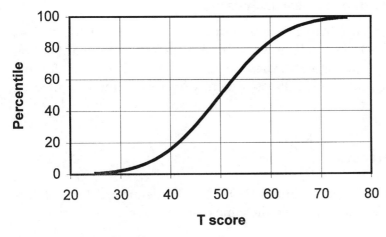

Figure 1.10   T scores to percentiles

In this chapter a variety of diagrams and concepts which are commonly employed in educational research are introduced. Bar charts, histograms and box-and-whisker plots are described together with examples from primary school data. Three statistical ideas (Confidence Intervals, Effect Sizes and correlations) have also been explained. These charts and ideas are used throughout the book which aims to describe the ideas in words and pictures rather than use mathematics.

For readers who would like to follow up some of these ideas, annotated references are given below and full details of the publications are provided at the end of the book.

Data display and basic statistics

Fitz-Gibbon and Morris (1978) This book is a clear popular introduction to educational statistics with helpful step by step guides for the newcomer.

1.7 Summary and suggestions for further reading

Tufte (1983) An excellent book that takes a careful look at a variety of ways of displaying data together with advice on the best ways to do it.

Velleman (1998) A multi media introduction to statistical concepts and ideas. It takes an innovative approach and whilst it is a little expensive it does provide an exciting and authoritative start. The CD is not aimed specifically at education.

More advanced statistics

Gardner and Altman (1989) A short test written for medics not educationalists which is very good on Confidence Intervals.

Hedges and Olkin (1985) An academic book that deals with Effect Sizes and leads on to meta-analysis.

Hopkins *et al.* (1996) For anyone who wants to teach themselves statistics this is an excellent work. It takes the reader from a standing start to quite a high statistical level. It is the ideal book for the autodidact containing self-assessment exercises at the end of each section.

Sex Differences

Campbell (1998) and **Kimura** (1992) Two academic articles that outline male/female differences in some detail.

Notes

1. The PIPS project is widely spread throughout England and although a number of schools come from further afield the results reported in this book are best regarded as being English. The schools were not chosen to form a 'representative' sample but they do involve whole LEAs from a wide variety of situations and geographical areas.
2. More accurately the Standard Deviation is found by squaring the deviations, then finding the average and finally square rooting the result. This gives a kind of average deviation called the root mean square.
3. The formula is $ES = \dfrac{\text{Mean } A - \text{Mean } B}{SD}$.

Chapter 2

Baseline and other assessments

Pupil assessment in primary schools has increased enormously within England over the last few years. This is likely to have had a profound impact on the way that teachers see their teaching and the way in which pupils are educated. It makes sense, therefore, to go back to the beginning and to think about different types of assessment and what they can reasonably be expected to do and not to do. This chapter looks first at the different forms of assessment available and then at ways in which the quality of the assessments can be established. It moves on to look specifically at baseline assessment and the research basis that is available to us when constructing such assessments.

2.1 Background

2.2.1 Formal and informal assessments

A major distinction that can be made is between the informal assessments of teachers and others as part of their day-to-day professional life and the more formal, deliberate assessments which become part of some structured system. Teachers, head teachers and others continuously assess. Indeed, it is almost impossible to be part of a system, or even to be a human being, and not to assess by making judgements, explicit or implicit, about the people or the systems within which one is working. On occasion, this informal assessment is put on a more formal basis. This occurs when, for example, teachers have to estimate the National Curriculum levels at which their children are operating. It might also be that formality is required within an appraisal situation or as part of an appointment or promotion procedure. In these circumstances informal assessments are called upon in a formal way.

2.2 Different forms of assessment

2.2.2 Subjective and objective assessments

The second major distinction, and one that looks at first sight as though it overlaps with the first, is between subjective and objective assessment. In a subjective assessment, a teacher or other assessor makes judgements on a professional basis about an individual, a situation, an organisation or part of it. In an objective assessment, the judgement is taken out of the hands of the assessor. Some pre-ordained criteria are laid down and there is either a mark or a level awarded according to some behaviour, written evidence, or observation. Now, there is a tendency to think of the informal teacher assessment as being necessarily subjective and of the formal assessments as being necessarily objective but this is by no means the case. For example, it might be that the assessor of a written piece of work, within a formal assessment, is asked to put a subjective judgement on the quality of writing. Conversely a classroom teacher might have in-house rules that lay down objective criteria which form the basis of informal behavioural assessment.

2.2.3 Norm-referenced and criterion-referenced

The third major distinction is between norm-referenced and criterion-referenced assessment. Norm-referenced assessment is assessment in comparison to other people. Selection for a sporting team to represent one's country is norm-referenced. The aim is to select the best. Criterion-referenced assessment is an assessment in comparison to a pre-set standard. The clearest example of a criterion-referenced assessment would be something like a driving test where rules are laid down beforehand. Drivers pass if they are able to do certain prescribed things.

It has often been pointed out that norm- and criterion-referenced testing are rarely met in their pure forms and that much testing is a hybrid. The assessments at the end of Key Stage 2, for example, were originally conceived of as being criterion-referenced. Then, as experience with the system built up, it became apparent that it was necessary to collect data on how well pupils were able to do the newly written tests before levels could be related to the marks. In other words it was found impossible to apply criterion-referenced principles in isolation.

When constructing the criteria for a criterion-referenced test norm referencing is essential. We might, for example, aim to describe a certain type of skill or procedural behaviour in mathematics with the intention of saying, 'if the child can do this then they can be awarded a level four'. But one could never decide how the level four should be described unless one knew something about a lot of children and information on the average child in that particular age group

Figure 2.1   The assessment hybrid

would be very useful indeed. In other words, hidden behind the criterion-referenced assessment is norm-referenced data. There practically never is a pure criterion-referenced assessment and it would be better to think of assessments as having degrees of norm or criterion referencing associated with them. This is illustrated in Figure 2.1.

It has long been the case that traditional national examinations such as A levels are based on both criterion referencing (assessed through the judgements of individual examiners) and norm referencing (assessed by looking at the distribution of marks). Since the 1991 Education Reform Act criterion-referenced assessment has dominated the rhetoric of statutory assessments in primary schools. Since then, the system of descriptors has produced mountains of documentation and enormously detailed descriptions of what might constitute one particular level in one aspect of the curriculum. This has largely been unwieldy. Even the idea that you can readily write a test to check a level descriptor proves to be problematic. Having written the test item, it turns out that children don't function in quite the way the assessor thought. The result of this situation has been the inevitable move away from pure criterion referencing to a mixture of criterion and norm referencing. This has resulted in unexpected delays in the announcement of cut-offs for certain levels as the data come in and judgements are made. It would seem that practicalities ordain that we need a hybrid. Practicalities and purity do not sit happily together – at least in assessments.

2.2.4 Cognitive, affective, behavioural and physical

We have then, three different categories into which we could place assessments. There is the informal/formal divide, the subjective/objective divide and norm/criterion referencing. Additionally we need to consider the type of activity that might be being assessed. We are going to distinguish between four types of outcomes that we might be assessing. Following that we will recall that there are some characteristics of individuals that are stable and there are those which vary from day to day or are short lived or situation specific. The four different outcomes that might be assessed are cognitive, affective, behavioural and physical.

Cognitive outcomes refer to outcomes to do with thinking such as reading, doing arithmetic, solving a practical problem or doing science. Affective outcomes concern feelings. They relate to attitudes. In this book we will consider attitudes towards school and self-esteem measures. Behavioural measures are just that. They are concerned with behaviour. It might be behaviour in the class or outside the class, behaviour in relation to others, towards oneself and so on. Physical measures concern height, weight, coordination, strength, as well as fine and gross motor skills.

2.2.5 Stable and transitory outcomes

There may be aspects of an individual's behaviour which are exhibited in a particular classroom with a particular teacher and rarely elsewhere. There may be other behaviours which some children display more or less all the time. Some individuals may be impulsive, some may be optimistic. Other feelings are situation specific. For example, feelings of elation naturally follow a lottery win. Cognitive aspects may also be particular or specific. Some things are held in the mind for short periods and then either lost or passed on to the long-term memory. The content of the short-term memory is essential to the moment but is ephemeral. The capacity of the short-term memory, on the other hand, is a more stable feature and this capacity varies from individual to individual.

In the classroom the task of the teacher is often to deal with short-lived aspects of learning. As a child learns to read, for example, the teacher will steadily probe the child's position on the road to fluent reading and aim to move forward from there. The child's position is constantly changing and it would make little sense to organise formal assessments on a daily or hourly basis and yet the teacher is making those informal assessments continually.

2.2.6 Formative and summative

Michael Scriven's thinking about different types of evaluation led him to formulate the distinction between formative evaluations (those designed to help a programme improve), and summative evaluations (those designed to pronounce judgement on the programme). This useful distinction has since been used within the assessment field, but as with so many dichotomies within education, real life evaluations and assessments are rarely purely formative or summative. They tend to be used for both purposes. Students who can adjust their plans according to its results use even such a clearly summative exam as A level in a formative way. Colleges and schools also use A level results in a formative way to improve their provision with the assistance of monitoring systems such as the A Level Information System (ALIS).

Rather than thinking of the assessments themselves as being formative or summative it may be better to regard them as providing information that can have a variety of uses. They can be used to make decisions of varying magnitude. When the decision is decisive in some way the assessment is being used summatively and when it is being used to adjust or refine it is being used formatively. This view makes it clear that it is the use to which assessments are put that makes the difference. This is important because there may be a tendency to think that the technical quality of an assessment can be reduced when it is to be used formatively. But formative adjustments can be decisive in people's lives just as summative assessments can. If decisions are to be made about people on the basis of an assessment then it should be of high quality.

It might be thought that diagnostic assessments are formative in their nature, but even here the assessment can be used summatively. Vital decisions may well be made about pupils following diagnostic assessment, just as an 11 plus test could be used formatively even though its original conception is clearly summative in nature.

2.2.7 Characterising assessments

Having established these major distinctions between the different types of assessment we can use them to characterise existing tests. For example, if we look at the statutory assessments of reading at Key Stage 2 we would say that they are formal, objective assessments based on a mixture of norm and criterion referencing. The test is in the cognitive domain and it is of a relatively stable characteristic of pupils.

On the other hand, the teacher who notices that a child arrives in the class in an agitated state, because of something that has happened during the last 12 hours at home, is engaging in informal assessment, based on subjective information. She is using a mixture of norm and criterion referencing and the judgement is situation specific and relates to the affective domain.

Now it is clear from the way we are talking that different types of assessment are going to be useful in different circumstances. This book aims to describe development during the primary years by focusing on formal assessments which are intended to give teachers useful information about individual pupils and about the class and school more generally. If this information is to be useful then it must relate to stable features rather than transitory or situation specific characteristics. The effort involved in formal assessments would simply not make sense if it generated ephemeral data. In order to be sure that this is indeed what is being assessed great efforts are made to ensure the reliability of the assessments.

2.3 *Reliability*

When assessing something that is supposedly a relatively stable characteristic, such as vocabulary or non-verbal ability, we need evidence that the assessment is consistent over a period of time. This evidence can be gained by using the same assessment on two different occasions with the same group of pupils. The correlation between the two assessments is known as the test-retest reliability and should be around 0.9 or higher. This measure tells us not only about the quality of the assessment itself but also about the construct being measured. If it proves impossible to develop a reliable measure then one should consider the possibility that the hypothesised trait or outcome needs to be reconceptualised.

It is possible to look at the internal consistency of an assessment. A test of spelling is often made up of a number of different items and a check on its internal consistency involves checking that the pupils' responses to different items give the same general message. One common way to do this is to calculate the correlation between pupils' scores on the odd and the even items of a test. A similar approach is used for attitude measures. The Attitude to School measure, which has already been discussed, was formed from the pupils' responses to seven statements about schools. If the scale had internal consistency then pupils who were positive in their responses to one item will tend to be positive to the other items. The internal consistency can be measured on a 0 to 1 scale and for the Attitude to School measures it was 0.8. Figures above 0.7 are satisfactory for the internal reliability of attitude scales.

The internal reliability is often the easiest form of reliability to check for the test developer but it should only be used for objective data. If an assessment is based on an individual's judgement then problems will arise. For example, many small judgements will often be made during inspections or in some baseline assessments. A check of the extent to which these agree with one another will often show high internal consistency. But this is only human. Once we have a good, or bad, view of something or someone we tend to carry that opinion over to other situations. The phenomenon is known as the halo effect and assessors have to be careful to avoid its problems. Whenever judgements are involved it is vital to look at the inter-rater reliability.

If two independent assessors observe the same activity or whatever is being assessed, and make their judgements, then we can make some estimate of the inter-rater reliability. Any assessment which involves judgement should only be used formally once the inter-rater reliability has been established and accepted as appropriate.

In developing a baseline assessment, or any other assessment, one needs to be confident that the assessment is reliable and the three forms of reliability described above form a solid base from which assessments can be developed. But they are not enough. Assessment can be reliable but consistently biased. It is at least conceivable that inspectors are consistent in their judgements of schools in tough neighbourhoods but they consistently fail to take into account the circumstances within which the school is working. It may also be that a reading test consistently produces low scores for the visually handicapped because the material is not appropriate. In both these cases it is the validity of the assessment that is being challenged and the assessments need to be revised. Reliability is the *sine qua non* of assessment but it is not sufficient.

2.4 Validity

Assessments should be checked and receive the approval of experts irrespective of the statistical evidence or its psychometric properties. The assessments should look as though they can do the job for which they are intended. This is referred to as 'face validity'. Some assessments look as though they are appropriate but turn out to have problems. One notorious example is the use of interviews to assess job applicants. This has repeatedly been shown not to be a good assessment of the suitability of applicants but continues to be widely used, often being given greater weighting than it deserves, presumably because face validity can be so persuasive.

How can we know that the interview is so poor? It is because later assessments of job performance are only weakly related to interview success. In other words the interview has low predictive validity. Many assessments are designed to predict the future in some way or other and whilst none can do so precisely it would be odd if they failed to do so entirely. If GCSE scores did not relate to A level grades then they should not be used to select students onto A level courses. If spelling scores one year were unrelated to spelling scores the next year then the formal assessment of spelling would be rightly criticised. If inspection reports of a school, separated by one year, were unrelated to one another it would be odd.

In thinking about predictive validity we must not make the mistake of dichotomising the issue. It is not a question of predict or not predict. It is a matter of 'to what extent' it predicts. Pupils change over time and it will never be the case that children's scores remain static and the same holds for institutions and people. They change but they change in a limited way. If a formal assessment does not relate to future assessments then it is of no value. One might just as well throw dice. Ephemeral characteristics are important and need attention but in an informal on-going manner.

Similarly we would expect that two quite different and independent assessments of the same thing would come up with more or less the same answer. A statutory test of spelling, for example, should, within reason, pick out the same children with spelling difficulties as does a purchased test. The extent to which the two independent measures agree is the concurrent validity. Together with predictive validity it provides stringent criteria by which assessments should be judged. A further piece to add to the jigsaw is construct validity.

All assessments, either implicitly or explicitly, have some idea or construct that is being assessed. This construct may or may not have been well thought out. A concept such as self-esteem, or self-concept, has been assessed on many occasions and many self-esteem instruments have been developed often with poor indications of validity. It would now seem that this is because the construct 'self-concept' is itself faulty and that it needs to be broken down into self-concept relating to the physical self and self-concept relating to academic matters. Then the academic part can be broken down into reading, mathematics and so on. Once this has been done, the way becomes open to reliable and valid assessments of the various sub-units of self-concept. This empirical work linked to theory now provides a firm basis for the assessment of self-concept and it provides an example of the way in which the background to an assessment can provide a coherent theoretical and empirical base. This constitutes construct validity.

Finally, in any consideration of assessment we should bear in mind the impact that the assessment has. Assessments are intended to improve things, or at a minimum simply to help study things and not make them worse in the process. Baseline assessment, for example, should help to provide a better education for the children being assessed. Inspections should improve educational provision and so on. In fact, in the last analysis impact is everything. If an excellent assessment had a negative impact it should be dropped. The only difficulty is that we will never know what impact assessments are having without good assessments – but that is another story.

2.5 Baseline assessment

We turn now to look more carefully at baseline assessment and start with its many purposes and the ways in which it might develop. Baseline assessment has a number of possible uses associated with it. Some of these purposes overlap with other assessments that are carried out at different ages but there are specific aims associated with on-entry assessments. This is being thrown into relief because of the introduction of compulsory baseline assessment in September 1999 within England. In Wales statutory baseline starts in September 2000 whereas there are different arrangements within Northern Ireland and Scotland.

Baseline assessment is something that teachers have carried out for years and there has been considerable research into the area with many efforts to set up baseline assessment systems in the past. It is a natural process for a teacher to assess the children when they first arrive at school. It is a way for her to get to know the pupils and it is needed to help plan the future for pupils in the classroom over the next week, term and beyond. There is also a need to begin to identify children with special needs. Some may be struggling in particular ways. Others may be unusually able. The baseline assessment can also be part of the interface between the teacher and the parents. The assessment can involve collecting information from parents, but others who have known the children in the past, either from nursery or from playgroup or other professional bodies, may also be important. There is also the possibility of feeding back information to parents and, interestingly, the information might all go back to the nursery or to the playgroup so that they could see how that child is progressing when he or she first goes to school.

Another important aspect, and one that has only come to the fore recently, is the possibility of assessing children when they first enter school in order to look at how they progress later on. Interest can focus on individual children and it will be important for the teacher to spot the child who fails to thrive. Alternatively, interest might be on the progress of the class as a whole, or possible sub-groups within the school. When we look at the progress of a whole class, or individuals in that class, in comparison to the progress of similar pupils elsewhere, then the interest is in Value-added measures and more space is devoted to that topic later.

Given this variety of purposes and given that we might be looking at cognitive, affective or behavioural aspects it seems that the baseline developer is in a daunting situation and we might wonder where to start. When we look at the different baseline assessments we see an enormous variety and one reason for that is surely that different people have had different ends in sight during the development and have therefore taken different approaches.

Clearly decisions have to be taken at an early stage about the main aims of the assessment. Within England the official criteria for accreditation of baseline schemes include two main purposes; one is to help the teacher plan the curriculum and the other is to lay down the basis for Value-added measures at a later date. The following few paragraphs outline the way in which one system (PIPS) was set up in order to create a baseline assessment.

The PIPS baseline assessment was set up in order to lay down the basis for looking at Value-added measures. If we had been looking to create a baseline to help plan the curriculum, then that would have taken us down a slightly different route, and if its purpose was identifying special needs then that would have involved a different route again. But it might also be that the baseline designed for Value-added purposes becomes useful for other purposes as well. Having created an assessment it then becomes possible to see how valuable it is for different ends, but those are only possibilities. One of the difficulties that arise with assessments is when they are asked to do jobs for which they were not intended. If one were to use a baseline assessment in order to allocate finance to a school but at the same time use the data in order to act as a basis for Value-added then we might find a little difficulty. If a teacher were asked to use subjective judgements to give a child a rating and that rating was going to determine how much money the school received then it might be that professionalism would be somewhat strained.

So having set out our stall, how might a baseline assessment be created in order to form a good basis for Value-added? Well, the first thing is that Value-added is going to be looking at the changes in pupils over time. The idea behind Value-added, which is considered in more detail later, is to compare like with like. We are going to take pupils that are apparently similar, on the baseline assessment, and then compare those children's achievements later on. So if we are going to be fair, we must compare children who have a similar starting point and that starting point must give some indication of how well they are likely to succeed in the future. In other words we must have a baseline assessment which is as strongly related to the children's later achievement as we can make it. One way of saying this is that it must correlate well with later outcome measures that we are interested in (predictive validity). It must clearly measure one or more stable characteristics of children on entry and the assessment must be consistently carried out from teacher to teacher and from school to school (reliability).

As far as children on entry to school between the ages of four and five are concerned that means that the baseline assessment must be related to later assessment at the end of Key Stage 1. So, we need to know what it is about young children that is related to their later success or difficulty. Success in this case means success in cognitive terms, in the National Curriculum, in English and in mathematics.

We need to know what it is about a young child when he or she starts school at four that will allow us to look at later progress. To find this out we could take many teachers' ideas and assess children on those different aspects. We would then wait until the children got to seven and see which ones were the best indicators. Fortunately, we don't have to do this. There have already been many longitudinal studies that have tracked children through from the age of four or five, up to the age of seven and beyond. We can look at those studies to see what best predicts early success. The work carried out by Peter Blatchford and co-workers is interesting here. He assessed children at the age of four in London nursery schools and then collected their London reading test scores at the age of seven. Others have carried out similar studies and several references to important pieces of work appear at the end of the book. They are listed briefly, with notes, at the end of this chapter.

The main points to come out of these pieces of research are that the following aspects have been shown to be reasonable predictors of later reading:

- Vocabulary. Language development is crucial, and the quickest assessment of language and the most reliable is a vocabulary assessment. Clearly this presents an issue for children whose first language is not English and this is considered later.
- Asking the child to write his or her own name or to copy a piece of writing.
- Marie Clay's Concepts about Print. Marie Clay suggests that before children learn to read they will recognise writing and reading when people do it. They will be able to distinguish writing from pictures and know what a letter is even though they may not be able to read it and so on.
- Letter identification is important although a sizeable proportion (between a third and a quarter) of children do not recognise any letters when they start school.
- Reading. Some children will be reading well on entry to school and it is useful to record this.
- Phonological awareness. The indicators of what are good predictors of later reading are very well researched indeed and more recently it has become clear that phonological awareness is an important variable. Indeed children who seem to be doing well in many other ways but are missing out on the ability to spot the on-set sound of words or the rhyming of words look as though they are likely to struggle at a later date. Fortunately, it is actually possible to remediate this to some extent.

Whilst there is an enormous amount of information available in relation to the prediction of reading the same cannot be said of mathematics. Although there has been important work, a surprising proportion of the writing about early maths is not based on follow-up studies but rather describes theoretical structures about what was important in developmental terms or on observation at one point in time. It is, however, clear that number is important. In the PIPS baseline we include:

- Ideas about maths. This includes concepts such as bigger, most and tallest.
- Counting. In the first versions we simply asked pupils to count objects in a picture, but we found that this was not a very reliable assessment and did not add much to the prediction of later cognitive success. Since then we have concentrated on counting a small number of objects, since failure to do that helps to pick out children likely to have continuing difficulties after the other baseline information has been taken into account. We have also introduced 'numerosity' – after children have counted four apples we hide them and then ask 'how many were there?'
- Early sums. At this stage, sums of the formal type, 'What is two plus four?', are inappropriate for most children although many children do succeed when the sum is presented using a different approach: 'Here are three balls, if I took one away, how many would there be?' It is interesting to note at this point that children starting school tending to find subtraction easier than addition. It is only after formal sums are introduced that this reverses.
- Digit identification.

We constructed a baseline assessment looking for a relatively stable measure of young children. The assessment is formalised so that everybody is working on the same basis and it is objective. The results are converted to a norm-referenced score.

They have to be objective because they are going to be used for Value-added purposes. If the children were assessed on one basis in one classroom and another basis in another classroom, the fundamental idea of comparing like with like would be undermined. To check on this we wait until pupils have been assessed in their schools and then we reassess some pupils at random ourselves. Using this reliability information we have refined the PIPS baseline assessment on a number of occasions. The test-retest reliability in 1998 was 0.93. This is very high indeed. Naturally some parts of the assessments are more reliably assessed than others. The most consistent is letter identification and the least is the rhyming section.

In refining the baseline we tried some assessments that did not work very well. For example we included the draw-a-man test, or rather, the more politically correct, draw-a-person test. This did not prove to be a good indicator of later success. We also employed factor analysis to see if the different parts that we had assessed were actually measuring different things or if they seemed to form one coherent structure. It turned out that all the different parts of the assessment, that is the vocabulary, the early reading, the letter identification and so on, seemed to measure a single underlying feature of the children. We might at this stage identify it as a general cognitive developmental level.

Interestingly in the factor analysis we found a second weaker feature from the items that might have been taught in a more formal way before school starts. This included some of the harder letters and digits, double-digit numbers and reading. This suggests that there is a small group of pupils who have been trained in formal reading and arithmetic and have learnt some specific skills.

Having carried out the baseline assessment at the time of entry to school we then waited until the children got to age seven and gave a reading and a maths test as well as collecting statutory results. We were then able to look back and see what parts of the assessment were important and what were not so important. The PIPS baseline assessment was then refined in the light of this exercise. An incidental finding of this research was that the Key Stage 1 results were not of as high a quality as one might hope. There seemed to be some inconsistency in the data from school to school. For Key Stage 1 data we found correlations up to 0.6 with the PIPS baseline assessment and against the PIPS reading and maths assessments we had a correlations up to 0.7. This is a high figure and probably about as high as can reasonably be expected between the ages of four and seven. It might be thought that the PIPS assessments at the ages of four and seven correlate well because they are similar assessments but in fact the PIPS Year 2 tests are quite different from the baseline. They are group assessments for seven-year-olds unlike the individual one to one assessment with the four-year-olds on entry.

It is worth noting at this point that any idea that it might be possible to create a group assessment of children aged four is quite erroneous. Many children at that age are simply not able to cope with the formal group discipline in the relaxed way that is necessary. In some observational work that we carried out there was one baseline assessment which was done on a group basis in one local authority. It was the only time that we have seen children upset doing a baseline assessment. We are keen that young children actually enjoy assessments and it is certainly our impression that most do.

Having developed a baseline assessment for Value-added, teachers have reported that they have found the information useful for their own classroom setting in planning and grouping pupils, amongst other things. This is a bonus and something that we have encouraged.

2.5.1 Personal and Social Development

So far we have concentrated on the cognitive aspects of baseline assessment. But affective and behavioural development is also important. In the initial stages of PIPS we did not address these issues but we have now created a Personal and Social Development part to the baseline and are in the process of looking at the physical side to the assessment as well. The way that it was done was to look at the literature on the development of children and to see what was thought to be important for the children's wellbeing and the way in which they might develop within the school situation. We also spoke to many Reception teachers and then constructed a draft assessment. Crucially, during the development process we asked two different adults working in the same classroom to complete the personal and social development inventory without talking to one another about it. This allowed us to compare the results and to see what aspects seemed to be consistently assessed between the two adults. Having done that, we then dropped items where there was considerable disagreement, kept those that could be identified reliably, and then looked to see which ones correlated with one another. Our aim was to have sections that did not correlate highly with one another. As noted earlier there is a real problem in doing a subjective assessment because we get a halo effect where a child is thought to be good in one way and therefore perceived to be good in another. When it comes to rating they always tend to get high ratings and another child who is perceived to have problems and difficulties then tends to get low ratings. This does not happen, of course, with objective assessment but it is almost inevitable with subjective assessment. With this in mind we have refined the Personal and Social Development part of the assessment and will continue to refine it in the light of experience and data.

2.5.2 Identifying special educational needs

A baseline assessment should also help teachers to start identifying children with special educational needs. Children develop rapidly at this age and they go through a variety of different stages. Some shoot away in some aspects of development and some hang back and then come forward later, making it impossible to pin down all but the most stable of the special educational needs that particular children have. This means that the way to identify special educational needs is to track children over time. Some will be identified as having special educational needs and then drop out of that category and others might remain with a statement for some time.

2.5.3 Communicating with parents

When children first arrive at school it is often the first major change in their lives. Parents too can find the change quite traumatic. They may well have devoted more than four years of their lives to the growing infant and now she or he is suddenly missing. It is not surprising that parents want to know how their child is getting on at school. Schools have a duty, and in England a legal necessity, to feed back information to parents on the baseline assessment.

When this was about to become a requirement we surveyed schools to see what they had been doing and found that it was quite common not to mention baseline assessments to parents. Those teachers who had talked to parents, however, had found the exercise to be a very positive one and we recommended that schools should adopt the following procedure, which is based on tried and tested practice.

Before the pupils start school it is a good idea for them to visit the school with their parent(s) or guardian(s). At that time it is appropriate to mention the baseline assessment and to show it to the parents. Then when parents visit later in the first term, they talk to the teacher individually. The parents are given a general picture of how their child settled in, what they have been doing, what they have enjoyed and what the school found out on the baseline assesment. This feedback can be couched in positive terms: phrases such as 'Jane did well on the vocabulary section but not so well on rhymes. We are working on rhymes with her now. Perhaps you could help with this at home'.

We advise schools not to give numbers to parents unless there are exceptional circumstances. We think that numbers can encourage unhealthy parental competitiveness. ('Mine got 65, what did yours get?') We also feel that numbers sound firmer and more permanent than they actually are. Teachers know that an assessment has some uncertainty associated with it and that children can change quite dramatically but parents do not necessarily know that, and it may be better to avoid going into details.

There are some parents who are well able to cope with standardised scores and who demand the numbers. In such cases teachers should tell all.[1] When doing so it is important that the teacher ensures that the limitations of the figure are made clear and that the other aspects of the child's development are given appropriate weight.

2.5.4 Children whose first language is not English

In one of the Local Education Authorities using the PIPS baseline assessment there are more than 100 languages which may be spoken among the children! This presents an apparently daunting task. Can one fairly assess children on the same assessment in different languages? Well, yes and no. This is one of the major challenges for baseline assessments and care must be taken. One thing should be made clear: if you cannot communicate with a pupil then you cannot assess. Fortunately this is very rare indeed. In most cases either the child knows sufficient English, or there is a bilingual teacher or assistant who can help.

Much of the PIPS baseline can be carried out in the child's own language be that Urdu, Vietnamese, British Sign Language or whatever and the CD version is translated into three languages other than English. Sections which can be carried out in any language include Ideas about Reading, Ideas about Maths, Counting and Early Sums.

There are some sections that can be carried out in different languages with varied levels of difficulty. Digit identification, for example, is appropriate for child speakers of certain languages but not for those languages where the written script involves different symbols for numbers. This is even more true of letter identification and writing.

Finally, there are two sections where the questions can be asked in the child's own language but where the key sounds or words are the same for all assessments. This holds for rhymes and picture vocabulary. Teachers need to teach children English, if they do not already know it, and it is useful to have a measure of baseline vocabulary. They must also teach the reading of English and the detection of the English rhymes is therefore important.

2.6 Summary and suggestions for further reading

The basic ideas surrounding educational assessment are covered in this chapter including the distinctions between formal/informal, subjective/objective as well norm/criterion-referenced assessments. It also outlines the various domains that might be assessed and describes the concepts of reliability and validity. The distinction between formative and summative approaches is outlined noting that the distinction is not a function of the assessment itself but the way in which the assessment is used.

Baseline assessments are considered in terms of the purposes that they serve and the research base that is available for their development. The evolution of one baseline assessment (PIPS) is recalled. Feedback to parents is considered as well as the identification of special educational needs and assessing children whose first language is not English.

Assessment

Black (1998) A very recent wide-ranging book that gives a well-received view of the assessment field.

Fitz-Gibbon (1996a) This prize winning book takes a broad view of assessment and its use within monitoring systems.

Hunter and Hunter (1984) An academic article which discusses the use of interviews as a predictor of job performance.

Marsh *et al.* (1988) An important academic article which deals with the development of self-concept measures.

Eysenck (1995) An interesting and unusual example of assessment is discussed in this book which discusses the validity of the concept 'genius' and the degree to which great figures can be reliably identified.

Baseline assessments

Lindsay and Desforges (1998) The authors provide an excellent recent overview of baseline assessment and include good sections on the technical quality of assessment as well as clear writing about special educational needs.

Wolfendale (1993) This booklet provides a clear review of the issues surrounding baseline assessments in a short work prepared for World Organisation for Early Childhood Education (OMEP).

Blatchford and Cline (1994) Under a series of headings this academic article provides a useful background against which baseline assessment may be considered.

The knowledge base on which baseline assessments can build

Blatchford *et al.* (1987) An academic study of the relationship between assessment in nursery and at the age of seven.

Goswami and Bryant (1990) A key text that deals specifically with phonological skills linked to reading.

Tymms and Williams (1996) A study, commissioned by SCAA, that deals with the potential of baseline assessment to act as a basis for Value-added. The report includes a set of references and a brief review of the literature in relation to predictors of later success or difficulty.

Tymms (1999) An academic study of the efficacy of a variety of baseline variables in the prediction of reading and mathematics.

Notes

1. By law, if data relating to an individual are kept on computer there is a legal right for the individual to have access to those numbers.

Chapter 3

Achievements and the differences between pupils

One feature that distinguishes humans from animals is our extraordinary capacity for learning. This learning exhibits itself in many fields, but perhaps its most astounding manifestation is in the acquisition of a language which happens during the preschool period for the vast majority of children. The refinement of language continues apace during their time at school. This acquisition and refinement involves not only the assimilation of the complexities of particular grammars with their accompanying rules of syntax but also the learning of new words. It has been estimated that children learn words at the rate of about ten a day during their primary school years.

This is such an awesome accomplishment that we can be very thankful that it does not depend on any curriculum devised by humans. Not only would the necessary documentation dwarf any national curriculum ever devised it would literally be an impossible task. Fortunately humans have an innate ability and tendency to acquire language. What we do as teachers is to capitalise on this natural ability and to help children on their way. The idea that parents and teachers somehow teach children how to speak is erroneous in the same way that it is a mistake to think that we teach children how to walk or how to breathe. Almost without exception children arrive at school with language already under their belt. Some of those children might be reluctant to use it when they first arrive in unfamiliar surroundings, but the idea that some children start school 'without language' is simply wrong. Similarly it is now clear that we develop the ability to do simple sums without being taught and that our minds are very active places indeed without the need for formal instruction or even language.

There are however, some things that are quite clearly taught. They are not instinctive. They are learnt by building on what has been acquired naturally. These include reading, writing, formal arithmetic, algebra, map work, and many other skills. They belong to the category of systems invented by humans. For example, the idea that one can write down a language using an alphabet of the sort we use

3.1 What pupils learn in primary schools

today in Britain stems from its invention by the Canaanites around 4000 years ago. It is not instinctive, it is a clever invention and although some pupils are able to pick up the names of letters without being taught them before they come to school, it is a system that needs to be taught. Some of these invented systems, like writing, are now so much part of our way of being that we regard their use as essential to modern life and schools are entrusted with transmitting this part of our culture. Some systems, such as calculus, are not regarded as essential but are nevertheless useful and are taught to volunteers (A level mathematics students) later in life. Yet other systems, such as Morse code, are no longer useful, and are only learnt by the inquisitive.

Schooling can be seen as a mixture of nurturing the natural development of children alongside the deliberate teaching of the invented knowledge and skills which are believed to be important enough to spend time on in school. Indeed the design of a school curriculum should be the result of carefully balancing these aspects of learning and relating them to the development of children. The curriculum should also balance the needs of individuals to function in society with the needs of society to have skills available to it. These issues can been seen surfacing in the debates over Early Years education. When is it appropriate to start to teach children our human inventions as opposed to nurturing their natural development through, for example, play? They continue to surface with discussion about the teaching of science and the extent to which it is possible to teach concepts or whether pupils must construct the concepts themselves. They also form the main debating point surrounding the teaching of academic versus practical subjects in the secondary school.

We can document the steady intellectual development of children but it is much harder to separate out the parts that have been deliberately taught from the parts that would simply have been acquired in any case. We also know that some children learn much more quickly than others but it is hard to separate out the effect of teaching from ease of learning. A later section on Value-added will attempt to do just that but we start with a simple description of the intellectual growth of children in primary school.

3.2 Vocabulary

The most straightforward measure of language development, and indeed of intellectual development more generally, is simply a measure of vocabulary. In Figure 3.1 the growth in vocabulary during the primary years can be seen. From entry to the school system at the age of four to the age of 11 in Year 6 and then 14 in Year 8[1] there is a steady rise. This rise represents an expanding vocabulary, which is tagged by exemplar words in the right hand column. On entry to school almost all children whose first language is English know the word 'carrots'. (They can readily pick out carrots from a picture when asked to do so.) On the other hand 'icicle' is much harder and only about half the children starting school can pick out an icicle when asked to when they first start school. In Year 2 about 75 per cent of children know the word and by Year 4 the vast majority know it.

The diagram has one other interesting feature. As we move from left to right and as the scores rise steadily the tops of the boxes rise more quickly than the bottoms. Similarly, the top whiskers rise more quickly than the bottom whiskers. To many teachers this is just the kind of thing that they know from experience but work hard to change. Children who start school with a relatively small vocabulary tend to fall further behind, in relative terms, as they mature. Conversely children who start with a more extensive vocabulary tend to extend it more rapidly than others.

The diagram would seem to confirm the biblical quote 'to him that hath shall be given'. But we need to recall that this diagram is a generalised picture and that individual children buck this trend. The vocabulary growth of individuals is much more varied than Figure 3.1 might suggest.

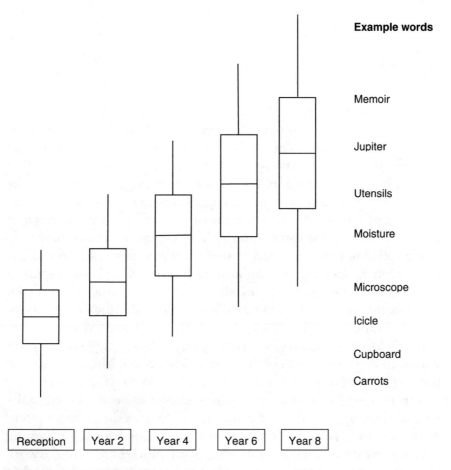

Figure 3.1 Vocabulary development

Most children arriving at school cannot read. About one per cent seem not to understand the terms reading and writing at all when they first arrive at school in England. About 30 per cent cannot identify a single letter although 20 per cent can read one letter (often the first letter of

3.3 Reading

their own name) and 3 per cent know all letters. The distribution of the number of letters known on-entry to school is shown below:

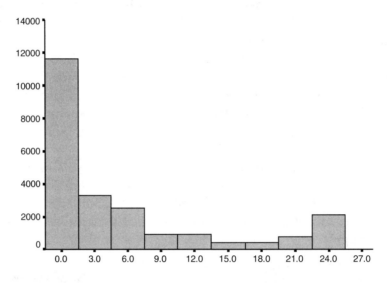

Baseline assessment: Letters identified

Figure 3.2 Letters identified on-entry

The U-shape of Figure 3.2 is very unusual in cognitive data and presumably corresponds to the way in which children are developing their understanding. When very young they have no concept of writing but at around the age of three some start to be aware that writing holds meaning and a few realise that there are marks on the page that have sounds. Once this stage has been reached and the first letter learnt the next letter is not far behind and then the floodgates open and the rest are learnt rapidly. This explains why we find very few pupils knowing just half the letters. Once they catch on to the idea of letters they don't hang around for very long knowing just a few of them. Some pupils know all the letters when they start school and around one per cent are reading sentences. But the experience of school combined with ageing soon changes all that. Within a year many children are reading a variety of words in simple sentences and within three years most children are reading well. This explosion is nothing short of miraculous and opens doors to the young mind.

This unsung national year on year success can be attributed to the natural developing ability of children and to our educational system at the heart of which is dedicated teaching. This teaching of young children to read is something to admire and much of the groundwork is carried out in reception classes. Unfortunately the reception teacher finds herself sandwiched between the early years preschool advocates, some of whom regret the existence of reception classes, and the National Curriculum pressures of Key Stage 1 and beyond. My own experience is that reception classes are excellent places of learning that are staffed by skilled dedicated teachers and peopled by happy young children with supportive parents. The caricature of classes of

35 pupils with a single teacher formally teaching four-year-olds to read before they are ready simply does not match reality.

The skills associated with reading can be split into two separate but essential parts – decoding and understanding. Decoding is the process of translating marks on the page into the sounds that they represent. Understanding involves taking the sounds and making sense of them. Of course, the two often go together. People who can decode well tend to be able to comprehend well also. But they are important and illuminating counter examples. Some pupils are able to decode well but have little understanding of what they read. Similarly there are pupils who can understand well but have great difficulty with decoding.

As an aside it is interesting to note a parallel with speech. It would seem that there is a specifically identified part of the brain associated with language. This part of the brain is distinct from the part(s) devoted to understanding. This suggests that it is possible to have good control over language but no comprehension or, conversely, to have good comprehension but no language. Amazingly small proportions of the population fit into just these categories. There are stroke victims who still retain their understanding and appreciation of the world but are frustrated by their inability to communicate since the language part of their brain has been destroyed. Others tragically develop with a good working language centre but little understanding. A fuller account of individual cases and the implications may be found in Pinker's book on the 'language instinct'.

Returning to the development of reading, it is clear that a teacher must be sensitive to the differing needs and developmental profiles of children. All teaching builds on previous experience and knowledge and the good teacher is sensitive to this within individuals while continually looking for opportunities to extend learning and experience. The enormous body of research on reading is beyond the scope of this book but we need also to remember that it is the teacher who is at the centre of the child's experience of learning to read and that the vast majority of teachers are very successful in teaching reading to the vast majority of children.

3.4 Arithmetic

The bumper sticker 'If you can read this thank a teacher' is largely accurate but a truer slogan would be 'If you can do sums thank a teacher'. Almost all of the formal mathematical knowledge of society is passed on through the education system. This is quite different from language development and schools do not have such a large influence on reading as they do on mathematics.

Children's mathematics starts before they enter school and there is good evidence to suggest that very young children (two years) have some understanding of number and that basic number concepts are universally found across cultures. It is the formalisation and extension of these basic ideas for which education is responsible. Figure 3.3 shows the general pattern of the growth of arithmetic skills of children from Year 2 to Year 8. The chart is based on group tests from PIPS and does not include anything from the on-entry assessment since it is very rare for pupils at that stage to have any knowledge of formal arithmetic, although many are adept at working with numbers in an informal way.

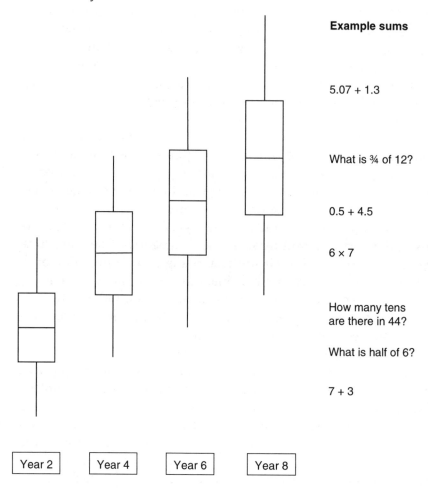

Example sums

5.07 + 1.3

What is ¾ of 12?

0.5 + 4.5

6 × 7

How many tens are there in 44?

What is half of 6?

7 + 3

| Year 2 | Year 4 | Year 6 | Year 8 |

Figure 3.3   Arithmetic development

The chart must be interpreted with care. When a pupil gets a sum right they may or may not have fully understood what they were doing. Bearing this in mind the general pattern for arithmetic matches the vocabulary chart shown earlier. The skills of the pupils rise steadily and there is a fan spread within the growth – the lower levels rise more slowly than the higher levels. About two thirds of Year 2 pupils can correctly say what half of six is, but the vast majority of pupils from Year 4 onwards have no difficulty with the question. On the other hand the sum:

$$0.5 + 4.5 =$$

is too hard a question for almost all seven-year-olds. By the age of nine about a quarter of pupils can do it, at 11 about half and by 13 the proportion rises to three quarters.

The skills of arithmetic and mathematics more generally are fundamental to our society and yet society has an ambivalent attitude towards them. Adults can boast about their lack of numerical ability but never about their inability to read. Steven Byers, while school standards Minister and encouraging schools to do more about numeracy, was able to answer '54' with impunity when asked to respond to the question 'what is seven eights?' He was later promoted!

Mathematics is also the poor relation of reading when it comes to research. The amount of work devoted to the study of reading is quite phenomenal when compared to the work carried out in mathematics. There have been important studies but much more is needed.

3.5 Science

If education can help adults to think scientifically then it will have fulfilled one of its major tasks. A scientific approach allows people to make sense of the physical world, to engage in reasoned discussions about vital activities in our society, to reject arguments based on belief or authority and to think systematically about evidence. Science has succeeded as no other discipline has ever succeeded. It has provided us with modern medicine, plastics, computers, surgery and telephones to name just a few. There is hardly any feature of modern life that does not owe its existence to science. It is also vital that children understand sufficient science to be able to make informed choices about their own lives, careers and hobbies. But within the PIPS project we have decided against assessing children's science in primary schools before Year 6. This is a policy decision that was not taken lightly.

Since science became part of the National Curriculum that had to be taught in primary schools there has been much splendid work in this area. But science in the sense of science as practised by scientists is based on a methodology that is not accessible to many pupils in primary schools. It requires thinking abstractly about what causes what. This needs careful measurement, observation and experimentation. The formal reasoning that underpins science requires thinking about variables and developing hypotheses, which can be tested. This position is backed by the work of Michael Shayer which suggests that most primary aged children have not reached a stage at which their cognitive development allows them to investigate situations involving more than one independent variable. This is a process that is fundamental to much of science. The capacity for this kind of thinking and problem analysis only gradually develops in young children and has its origins in curiosity.

Many successful scientists spent time when young thinking about the natural world, being fascinated by the working of machines or trying to make things. Isaac Newton flew kites at night with lighted candles inside them to the amazement of locals. Richard Feynman fixed radios by thinking and George Washington Carver sought out an education so that he could know 'what made hail and snow and whether a person could change the colour of a flower by changing the seed'. It is vital that this curiosity, play and sense of awe is developed or, at the very least, remains unharmed. The point is that there is a stage before *formal* science which involves the encouragement of interest and curiosity and which includes experimentation in an informal sense, which is a natural extension of play. There is a fear that attempts to test formal science before children are ready could be counterproductive.

But over and above the need to maintain curiosity and awe there is a major difficulty with testing science at an early stage. We are in danger of testing factual knowledge or asking reasoning questions divorced from science. The early attempts to test science at the end of Key Stage 1, which went for authentic tasks, met with something short of success (remember floating and sinking?) Further, the test results from those science assessments added nothing to the prediction of the end of Key Stage 2 science success after English and mathematics have been taken into account.

It seems better to downplay the formal assessment of science in primary schools and to look for key teaching approaches that can encourage the vital thinking skills of young children whilst fostering the natural enthusiasm for nature, construction, deconstruction and the reading of non-fiction. But whilst this perspective is honestly held it is appropriate to admit ignorance. There is a lack of research into the impact of introducing science to young children in different ways, and we do not know for sure if the formal testing of science in primary schools has any impact on pupils' attitudes to science later in life. We need to know more and the issue of gaining evidence for policies is taken up in the final chapter.

3.6 Non-verbal ability

One crucial aspect of children's development, which often goes without mention, is the speed at which they operate. This has enormous implications for life in the classroom and on a daily basis as well as for what might reasonably be expected of schools. Within the PIPS and PIMS projects pupils in Year 2, Year 4, Year 6 and Year 8 complete a timed test known as Problems of Position (POP). David Moseley, Reader in Applied Psychology at Newcastle University, devised the test. He was interested in the part played by visualisation and the accurate mental processing of spatial information in children's learning. Pupils are asked to join up the dots on the left-hand side of a diagram and then to find the same pattern of dots on the right hand side and join them up. They are not to choose patterns that are turned around or manipulated in any way. Two examples follow:

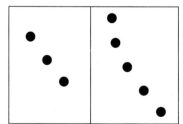 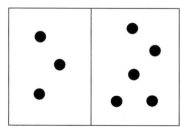

The problems can be very simple with little to attend to in the diagram, as in the first example, and they can get quite complicated. But the major challenge is to do as many as you can in the time available. We find this to be a useful assessment within the project because it is quick, it yields a reliable measure of pupils' ability to work speedily through problems that they have never seen before and it can be explained simply. It also has the advantage that, in collaboration with David Moseley, we have been able to develop the assessment without compromising the basic idea so that it is suitable for children from the age of 7 to 13 across the full range of ability. Because the assessment does not involve language *per se,* and because it requires mental effort to complete, we refer to it as a non-verbal ability test. The non-verbal part of the assessment allows teachers to have some additional insight into pupils whose first language is not English.

The diagram that follows (Figure 3.4) plots the number of items that pupils manage to do per minute in four year groups. The diagram is linked directly to the Durham data but as with the vocabulary and arithmetic diagrams a certain amount of interpretation was needed in its construction. The items employed in the tests are generally harder for the older pupils and as a result the patterns shown in the figure

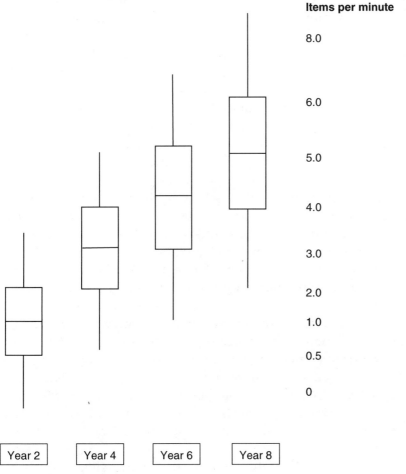

Figure 3.4 Non-verbal speed

probably underestimate the trends shown. That said, the general pattern shown in the diagram has a firm foundation and it is fixed by the results obtained from thousands of pupils.

Figure 3.4 shows a big variation amongst pupils within any one year group. In Year 6 for example pupils on the 25th percentile worked at the rate of about three items per minute but at the 75th percentile they were working at about five per minute. This is an important variation which teachers must take into account when working with their classes. Not only do some pupils more quickly work by themselves but also when listening to others they comprehend more rapidly. The difference is even more important at more extreme percentiles. The diagram suggests that there will be some pupils in Year 6 classes within the mainstream who work at more than twice the speed of others. It also suggests that some children in Year 2 are 10 times quicker than others in the same year group. The greater difference in Year 2 than in Year 6 seems paradoxical at first sight since the spread of scores is less. But in the same way that a single year for a four-year-old is more important than a year for a ten-year-old a small increase in speed makes a greater percentage difference for younger children.

Even larger differences are clear across the full primary age range. Although we do not have data for children before the end of Key Stage 1 the diagram can be used to make extrapolations. These suggest that between the start of Key Stage 1 and the end of Key Stage 2 the average pupil increases the speed at which he or she works eight-fold. Even more remarkable is the thought that some children at the end of primary school might be more than 100 times faster than some children at the start of their compulsory primary education.

The diagrams also show very clearly the overlap between age cohorts.

3.7 Age

In England many children start school in the September following their fourth birthday even though the law says that they only have to start in the term after their fifth birthday. This means that children can differ by more than a year on entry to school. The histogram in Figure 3.5 shows the age in months on 1 September 1997 of a large representative sample of pupils starting school in Reception in England in the autumn term.

The vast majority of pupils were aged from 4 years 0 months (48 months old and born in August 1994) to 5 years 0 months (60 months old and born in August 1995) inclusive. A very small proportion of pupils who started school in the autumn was older than this – some aged up to 5 years 6 months – and they are not shown on the figure. It would seem, judging from the chart, that about half of the parents of children aged just 48 months wait for a year before sending their children to school. The other interesting feature is the slight rise in percentage from left to right across the chart. This is probably accounted for by pupils who start school after Christmas and after

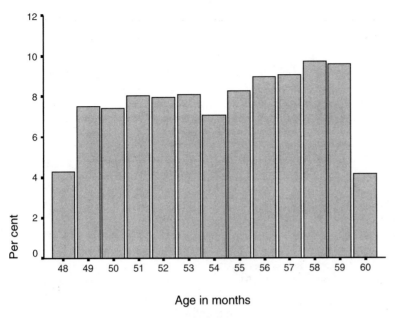

Figure 3.5   Distribution of ages on-entry

Easter. Presumably parents are more inclined to delay their children's start in school when they are younger. (Quite why there should be a drop for the proportion of children aged 4 years and 6 months is not clear.)

The situation then is quite complicated. Children start school at different ages and in different terms. But how much difference does age make to children's school based learning? The PIPS baseline standardised scores for children by month of birth are shown in the Figures 3.6 and 3.7. The first gives box-and-whisker plots and the second shows the same data by displaying the average score for each month of birth together with Confidence Intervals.

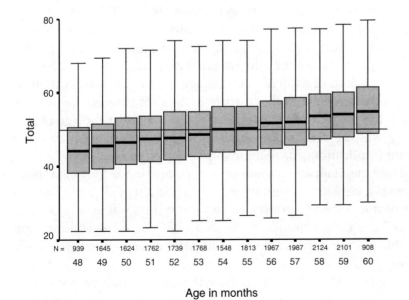

Figure 3.6   Baseline scores by age

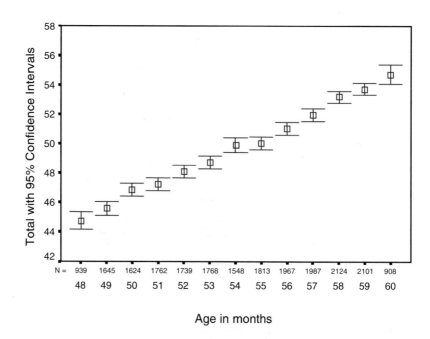

Figure 3.7 Baseline averages by age

There is a steady rise in scores by month of birth and the rise is quite steep. The difference in starting points for the average child aged 4 years and 0 months is about a Standard Deviation (Effect Size = 1) lower than an average pupil age 5 years 0 months. The steady rise of the chart shows that when parents decide to delay sending their young four-year-olds to school for a year it is not because their child is a slow developer. If this were the case the average score for 48 months would be higher than it is and the one for 60 months would be lower. As it is the averages fall more or less on a straight line.

The general increment by age is a very important feature of the Reception class but as pupils get older the importance of age decreases. The differences by month of birth are of greatest significance on-entry. At this early stage a year is a quarter of the life of a four-year-old. By the end of primary education it is just a tenth.

Another important association with age is physical size. Although this book does not look at this feature in detail it is worth bearing in mind that the August born child who enters school at the age of just four may well be one of the smallest in the class. This may have important implications for relationships with others.

But while the diagrams show the importance of age they also show that there is a very great overlap between children of all ages. The top quarter of the youngest groups scored more highly than the bottom quarter of the oldest group. As with all categories of children the crucial thing is the individual child rather than the category to which they belong.

We have seen in earlier charts how the cognitive development of children grows through the primary age range and it might seem as though age is crucial to this development. It most certainly is but it interacts with schooling and the progress that children make can be related both to the age and the amount of time that they have spent in the classroom. Children learn schoolwork during term time and tend to forget it during the holidays. A number of researchers have investigated this phenomenon and the general pattern of growth is shown in Figure 3.8.

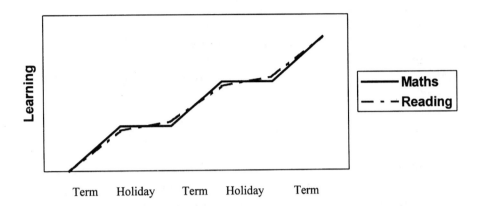

Figure 3.8 Pattern of growth

The general picture is that children learn during term time and then stagnate during the holidays. Overlaid on this general pattern are some interesting features. Some aspects of learning are more readily lost during the holiday than others. Arithmetic skills and spelling tends to be the hardest hit whereas conceptual knowledge appears to be longer lasting with holidays having less impact.

Another interesting feature, which is not shown in the diagram, is that school tends to reduce the reading inequalities in society and that holidays tend to exacerbate them. Generally children from lower socioeconomic homes lose the relative ground that they have made up in reading during the term and the reverse happens for the higher socioeconomic children. These effects are quite small but have been replicated in several studies.

3.8 Sex

Whether we were born male or female dominates the whole of our being. It has implications for our lives and loves as well as for our position and status in society. It is not surprising therefore to find considerable interest in the differences between the educational success of girls and boys. This is reflected in the many articles that can be seen in the press and official reports. (It is a requirement that the English baseline results must be broken down by sex.) One might be forgiven for thinking that sex was the dominant variable when the achievement of pupils in school is considered.

There are, of course, always differences between girls and boys on anything that one cares to name, and, if we are dealing with large numbers of pupils then the differences, however small, inevitably turn out to be statistically significant. The important question to ask, however, is not 'are there differences?' but 'how big are the differences?' We should also ask if the differences are simply found for averages or if there are differences at the extremes. For example, it might be that on average boys and girls are equally well behaved but that the best-behaved pupils are boys and the worst-behaved pupils are boys. Our approach, then, will be to consider the different measures and to ask how big the differences are between the sexes and if there are differences in the spread of scores for girls and boys. Probably the best way to do this is to look at box-and-whisker plots and an overview is provided by starting with pupils on-entry to school and to look at pupils in the last year of their primary education.

3.8.1 On-entry assessment

Overall the box-and-whisker plot in Figure 3.9, of the PIPS baseline, shows very little difference between girls and boys. The average was slightly higher for girls and the Effect Size was just 0.1 which is a long way from being educationally important and certainly not the kind of thing that would be noticeable in the classroom. In truth the most striking feature of the box-and-whisker plot is the remarkable similarity between the two sexes. But might it be that the various components of the assessment show up differences more clearly?

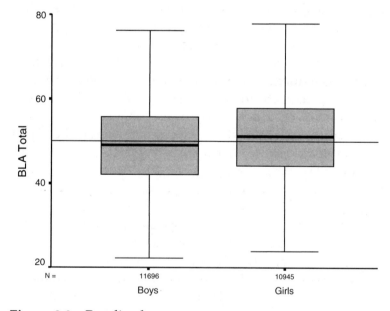

Figure 3.9   Baseline by sex

Table 3.1 shows that even for the sub-scales the male/female differences are small. The Effect Sizes are 0.2 or lower. The table also shows an interesting difference in the spread of scores for boys and girls on maths. The boys' scores are more heterogeneous. This suggests that the highest scores are more likely to be those of boys as well as the lowest scores. A similar result was reported recently in High Schools mathematics results in the United States. The difference in Standard Deviations is, however, slight and the differences at the extremes are not very apparent.

Table 3.1 Baseline scores and sex

Variable	Effect Size (in favour of girls)	SD boys	SD girls
Total	0.2*	9.9	9.9
Early reading	0.2*	9.9	9.9
Early maths	0.1*	10.2	9.6*
Rhymes	0.1*	9.1	9.1

* p < .01[1]

[1]This notation may be read as saying that the result was 'statistically significant at the 1% level'.

All of the subsections from the PIPS baseline showed statistically significant differences between boys and girls but none was large enough to be regarded as educationally important.

Two of the best predictors of later success are letter and digit recognition and for males and females these two measures were very similar. On average the girls knew 6.4 letters and the boys 5.0.[2] Of the ten digits the girls identified 7.1 and the boys 6.8. The Effect Sizes were 0.2 and 0.05 respectively. It would seem that the differences in girls' and boys' starting points in school are very small. There is a difference in that the girls were slightly ahead but it was only just detectable.

3.8.2 Year 6

Amongst the cognitive measures available in Year 6 (maths, reading, science, vocabulary and non-verbal ability) the biggest differences between girls and boys were in reading and non-verbal ability. Reading was in favour of girls and non-verbal ability in favour of boys. Figure 3.10 confirms that the differences were small. The Standard Deviations were significantly different for only two measures. The spreads were slightly smaller for girls in science and mathematics.

Table 3.2 Year 6 results and sex

Variable	Effect Size (in favour of girls)	SD boys	SD girls
Reading	0.2*	10.0	9.8
Mathematics	0.0	10.1	9.8*
Science	0.1*	10.2	9.7*
Non-verbal ability	−0.2*	9.9	9.7
Vocabulary	−0.1*	9.9	10.0

* p < .01

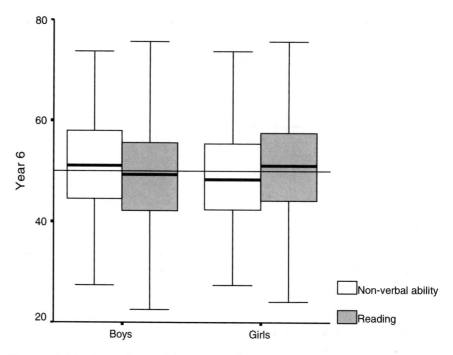

Figure 3.10   Year 6 cognitive scores by sex

These rather negative findings may be a surprise to some readers. Surely the papers are full of the differences between boys and girls and there have been recent reports of large differences in some baseline assessments. There are three points to be made here. The first is, as has already been noted, that there is always some difference between girls and boys. We could have presented the data in ways which made much of the statistically significant differences, but this book focuses on the size of the difference and that is small. The second is that the use of teacher judgement rather than objective assessments is likely to result in exaggerated differences between groups. No matter how careful humans are they tend to be biased in some way or another and our tendency to see pupils who are good in one way as being good in all ways (the halo effect) is well documented.

The third important reason is that male/female differences vary according to the nature of the assessment and the subject matter being assessed. The Year 6 reading test used in PIPS involved multiple choice answers about non-fiction. Were we to have asked for extended responses in relation to stories about human relationships we might well have found larger differences in favour of girls.

3.8.3 Behaviour

This chapter concerns the attainment of pupils but it also concerns differences between girls and boys and it is appropriate to include here the greatest difference that we have found between boys and girls. It is on a measure of behaviour at the end of the Reception year.

At the end of Reception many teachers in the PIPS project choose to complete a section relating to Attention Deficit Hyperactivity Disorder (ADHD). This is a syndrome associated with a tendency to fidget, lack attention and an inability to settle to any one activity. It is a controversial area and some have suggested that it is an artificial construct created to explain why some pupils behave oddly with some teachers. No doubt pupils' behaviour does vary according to the teacher that they are with, but there can be little doubt that for some children ADHD is a thing that they live with over the years. They exhibit similar behaviour with all teachers and at home. And, for some unusual children, it dominates their lives and it is not a topic that should be treated lightly.

In comparing the ADHD scores of boys and girls at the end of Reception Figure 3.11 shows something dramatic. Half of all pupils scored zero on the scale. Some pupils scored quite highly and that group was predominately boys.

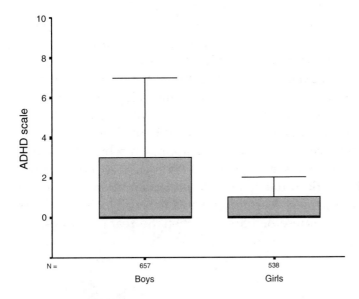

Figure 3.11   ADHD by sex

Table 3.3   Attention Deficit Hyperactivity Disorder and sex

	Effect Size (in favour of girls)	SD boys	SD girls
ADHD	−0.46*	2.5	1.7*

* p < .01

The average difference between the sexes is modest (Effect Size 0.46), but that average difference needs to be considered in conjunction with the Standard Deviations. The boys' scores are much more divergent than the girls' scores. At the extreme end of the scale the high scores are five times more likely to be those of boys. It would seem possible that this very great difference between the behaviour of boys and girls has some bearing on the large differences that appear between boys and girls when judgement scales are used for other variables. Halo effects carry over.

3.9 Home background

Primary schools in Britain are segregated. They largely serve local communities and often schools take pupils from the surrounding council estate, or expensive private housing or whatever. There are, or course, exceptions. A small village school, for example, might expect to take in pupils from a wide variety of backgrounds, as might a school that finds itself placed on the border of differing types of housing. But it is more common to find segregation and it is an important feature of our society and the educational system. It often dominates our perceptions and thinking about differences between schools and pupils.

In order to get a handle on the importance of home background it is necessary to measure it in some way and traditionally researchers have used the occupation of parents, often exclusively the father, to categorise families. An alternative approach is to use the family income as a measure or the mother's level of education, whilst others have used the Census data to get a measure of the neighbourhood in terms of car ownership, crowding in the home, telephone ownership among other variables. In the baseline assessment we collect data on the free school meal entitlement of pupils but in the Year 6 part of the PIPS project we have taken a different approach which involves a measure of home derived from pupils' responses in a questionnaire. This follows the work of the secondary projects in the CEM Centre, the educational researcher Alison Kelly and the sociologist Bordieux. The baseline data are presented first and then the Year 6 findings.

3.9.1 On-entry

Table 3.4 and Figure 3.12 show that the difference between those who receive free school meals and those who do not is modest on entry to school. The Effect Size is greatest for the early reading part of the assessment (0.7) and a little less for early maths (0.5). The box-and-whisker plot for the total score on the assessment shows this

Table 3.4 Baseline scores and free school meals (FSM)

Variable	Effect Size (in favour of no FSM)	SD no FSM	SD FSM
Total	0.6[*]	9.4	9.3
Early reading	0.7[*]	9.3	9.3
Early maths	0.5[*]	9.6	9.8
Rhymes	0.3[*]	8.9	8.1[*]

[*] p < .01

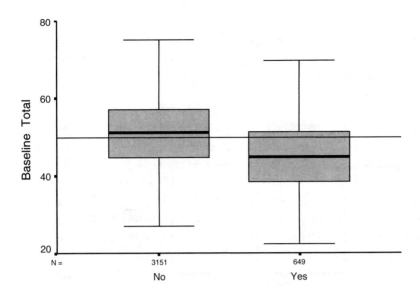

Figure 3.12   Baseline by free school meals

difference clearly but reminds us also of the great overlap between the two groups. There are many children from deprived circumstances who start school at a high level and vice versa.

3.9.2 Year 6

At the end of their primary education we ask pupils to respond to a series of statements about their background including one about books in the home and another about visits to art galleries and museums from home. These questions are used to create a scale, which gives a direct measure of the children's perspective of home known as Cultural Capital. The correlations of various outcome measures with Cultural Capital are shown in Table 3.5. A column is also included to show how the correlation converts into an Effect Size. The results for the curriculum based achievement scores are shown in Figure 3.13.

The table and charts show a clear but modest connection between Cultural Capital and achievement. For individual pupils the relation-

Table 3.5   Correlations with Cultural Capital in Year 6

Variable	Correlation	Effect Size
Reading	0.27*	0.6
Mathematics	0.23*	0.5
Science	0.24*	0.5
Non-verbal ability	0.12*	0.2
Vocabulary	0.24*	0.5

*p<.01

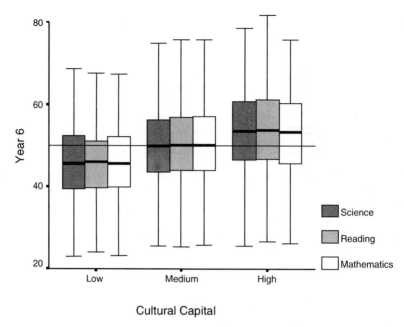

Figure 3.13   Year 6 achievement by Cultural Capital

ship is similar to that found with the baseline data using free school meals. The connection is strongest in relation to tests with a high verbal requirement and weakest for the non-verbal assessment. Overall the relationships may be described as weak to modest. But for a whole school the connection can be strong. If all the pupils come from one type of home then the weak relationship seen here at the pupil level becomes magnified into something dramatic. This has important implications. Teachers dealing with individual children can gain just a modest amount from a general knowledge of pupils' homes but much can be understood about a whole school by knowing about the general intake of pupils.

3.10 Developed ability

Teachers know that some pupils make more rapid progress than other pupils. The capacity to think more quickly, solve novel problems, understand and learn rapidly can be termed 'developed ability'. This construct can be distinguished from academic attainment that is, for example, exhibited by success in maths or science tests. Developed ability indicates a capacity to learn whereas attainment is the level of achievement that has been reached.

Table 3.6   Correlations with developed ability in Year 6

Variable	Correlation	Effect Size
Science	0.71[*]	2.0
Reading	0.67[*]	1.8
Mathematics	0.68[*]	1.9

[*]p < .01

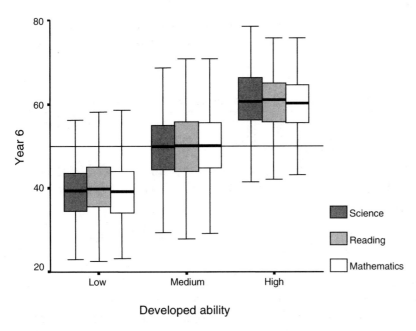

Figure 3.14   Year 6 achievement by developed ability

When considering the achievements of pupils it is important to look at developed ability measures. Within the data being examined here a combination of the picture vocabulary and non-verbal ability tests give a good measure of developed ability. Table 3.6 and Figure 3.14 show how this combined measure relates to attainment.

The relationships are easily the strongest that we have seen so far. Pupils who have the capacity to comprehend quickly generally have higher levels of attainment. This is a crucial feature of schooling and has important implications for comparisons of schools. Those schools that admit more able pupils will tend to get better attainment results (A levels, GCSEs and Key Stage results).

The term chosen here is 'developed ability' and it is important to emphasise that this term has no implications for the origins of this variable. Educational research has, on occasions, backed itself into a corner by spending time on the nature/nurture debate and other less savoury arguments. Developed ability is influenced by culture and although the non-verbal assessment is culture reduced it is by no means culture free.

The measures must therefore be treated with care but it is vital that we recognise the very great differences that are seen between pupils and recognise that these differences have important implications for the progress rates that can reasonably be expected of different pupils.

3.11.1 On-entry

3.11 First language

The issue of assessing pupils whose first language is not English, when they first start school, has already been discussed. Some data from such assessments are presented here and some care must be taken in interpreting the results. This is especially true for the baseline data, which were, on occasions, collected in a language other than English.

Table 3.7 Baseline scores and English as an additional language

Variable	Effect Size (in favour of English first)	SD English first	SD other
Overall	0.7*	9.8	12.1*
Early reading	0.8*	9.6	12.9*
Early maths	0.5*	9.9	11.0*
Rhymes	0.4*	9.1	8.2*

* p < .01

Table 3.7 shows the difference between the children whose first language is and is not English amounts to an Effect Size of about 0.7. The difference is greater for the early reading section than the early maths section presumably because it is more directly related to language *per se*. Greater Standard Deviations are associated with the pupils whose first language was not English. This suggests that although the average scores of that group are lower it includes pupils with very high and very low scores. This is confirmed in Figure 3.15.

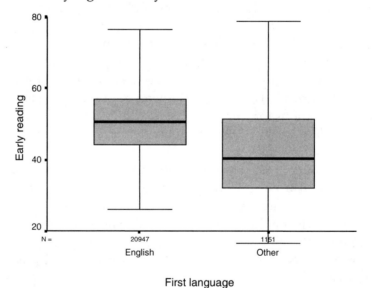

Figure 3.15 Basline reading by first language

3.11.2 Year 6

In Year 6 the assessments are all carried out as group tests in English. The pupils are asked which language they spoke first – English or something else. Their responses to that question were used to produce Table 3.8 and Figures 3.16 and 3.17. For the curriculum-based material (reading, maths and science) the difference amounts to an Effect Size of about 0.6 which is similar to that found for the baseline

Table 3.8 Year 6 scores and English as an additional language

Variable	Effect Size (in favour of English first)	SD English first	SD other
Maths	0.5*	9.7	9.8
Reading	0.6*	9.7	9.3*
Science	0.7*	9.7	9.0*
Non-verbal ability	0.3*	9.6	9.7
Vocabulary	0.9*	9.3	8.9

* p < .01

assessment. However, the curriculum-free material shows a different pattern. The vocabulary scores showed a greater discrepancy with an Effect Size of 0.9 whilst the non-verbal ability Effect Size was just 0.3.

Clear conclusions can be drawn from these data. The general pattern of assessment results for children whose first language is not English is one of under-achievement. This is strongly linked to their facility with English and not to their cognitive ability. This has important long-term implications. Under-achievement at this stage is likely to be followed by low school exit qualifications (GCSEs), less chance of higher qualifications and poor job prospects.

The solution to this problem must lie in education and in particular in the acquisition of English at an early stage. There are several parts of the country where this is already being given a major priority but more needs to be done. However, although the pattern and some conclusions are clear, a word of caution is also in order. The classification of pupils into first language groups was dependent on their ticking of boxes. It is quite possible that some children whose first language was not English but who felt very much at home with the language chose not to tick the box that indicated that their first language was not English.

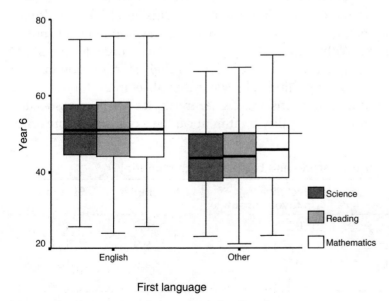

Figure 3.16 Year 6 achievement by first language

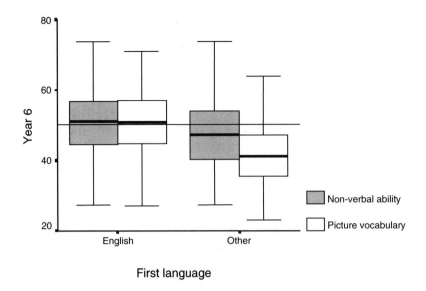

Figure 3.17   Year 6 curriculum-free scores by first language

3.12 Twins and higher multiple births

Twins and higher multiple births are becoming more and more common. In 1995 1.4 per cent of maternities resulted in a multiple birth and one in 35 children born was a twin or higher multiple. This incidence has been increasing since the early eighties as a result of both the increasing ages of mothers and fertility treatment. Improved care for premature and lightweight babies has ensured that twins and higher multiples form a higher proportion of the school population than ever before.

Twins and higher multiples are different from singles in many ways. They tend to be born prematurely, to be of lower than average birth weight and there is a higher incidence of complications at birth. Twins and higher multiples often form a particularly close relationship with one another and even on occasion develop their own language.

Research in the past has indicated that twins and higher multiples tend to lag behind singles in their reading development but not in mathematics. Within the PIPS project we have only found slight evidence of any delayed development in their starting points. This was a surprise; with hindsight we rationalise it as follows. The increased numbers of twins and higher multiples has been associated with older and, since fertility treatment can be expensive, more afflu-

Table 3.9   Baseline scores and twins and higher multiples

Variable	Effect Size (in favour of singles)	SD singles	SD twins
Overall	0.2*	10.0	10.1
Early reading	0.2*	9.9	10.0
Early maths	0.3*	9.9	10.1
Rhymes	0.1	9.1	9.2

* p<.01

ent mothers. The children of older or more affluent mothers tend to do better at school. We therefore think that the slight academic disadvantage of twins and multiples is just being offset by the advantages of being born to older more affluent mothers. This is, however, speculation and more work is needed in this area.

Table 3.9 summarises the latest results.

We have already noted that pupils are not evenly distributed among schools. They go to neighbouring schools or to schools that they or their parents choose, or that they have been selected for. This segregation of pupils is a major feature of the English educational scene. It has implications for the public perception of the system and often for politicians' perceptions. When league tables show massive differences between schools in the percentage of pupils getting a level 4 or above at the end of primary school there is a feeling that something must be done. The next chapter is devoted to looking at how fairer assessments can be made of school performance but in this chapter it is useful to look at the differences between schools on their baseline scores. Figure 3.18 shows the average baseline scores for 53 schools chosen at random from a nationally representative sample.

3.13 Schools

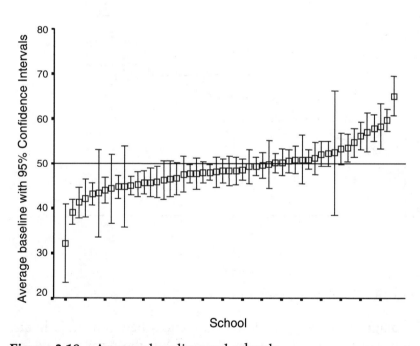

Figure 3.18   Average baseline and schools

The chart shows that schools take in pupils with very different starting points. Although many schools had average scores close to 50 there were some that had much higher and some much lower scores. The Confidence Intervals also varied from school to school and this is largely due to the differences in the numbers of pupils entering each

Table 3.10 Baseline scores and differences between schools

Variable	Effect Size
Overall	0.9*
Early reading	0.9*
Early maths	0.7*
Rhymes	0.7*

* p < .01

school in September. For some rural schools this can be a single pupil whereas others might have a three-form entry. We can summarise the school differences with Effect Sizes and these are listed in the Table 3.10. These are some of the largest Effect Sizes[3] that we have seen so far in this chapter.

The box-and-whisker plots in Figure 3.19 show five schools each of which have at least 30 pupils on intake. The central one has an average score. The ones to either side of the central one are one school-level Standard Deviation above and one below. The outer two are two school-level Standard Deviations away.

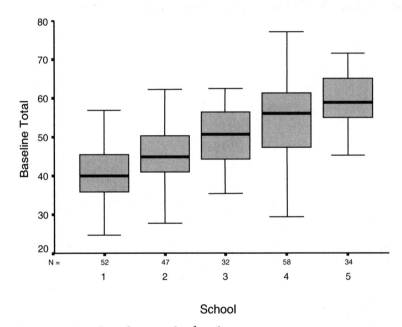

Figure 3.19 Baseline and schools

The diagrams show very large differences between the schools. Not only are the average scores different but the pupils at the extremes are very different. In school 1 there are no pupils starting school with high scores – there are no pupils reading when they start school for example, but there is a clutch of pupils starting with very low scores. Quite the opposite obtains in school 5.

This difference between schools when pupils start cannot be due to the schools themselves. The pupils were assessed within a few weeks of their arrival.

The rapid intellectual growth of children during the primary years is outlined in this chapter. The explosion of language is quite astonishing, as is the very rapid way in which children learn to read in school. Arithmetic also exhibits a steep learning curve and is paralleled by the increasing speed at which children can process new information. This intellectual growth is associated both with ageing and with schooling. The importance of both is emphasised.

By looking at information at different times during primary schooling the differences between the achievements of various groups are explored: boys and girls, pupils coming from different home circumstances, singles, twins and higher multiples, children with different first languages and pupils attending different schools. In each case emphasis is placed on the magnitude of the differences found. Large differences were found between schools and this is largely explained by noting that they serve segregated communities.

A distinction is made between pupils' developed ability and achievement and this is emphasised as being important in looking at the differences between schools. The strongest relationships found in the data were between developed ability and achievement.

3.14 Summary and suggestions for further reading

Cognitive growth

Pinker (1994) A wonderfully broad ranging book which provides a wealth of well-presented detail. (The reference to vocabulary acquisition can be found on page 150.) The main thrust of the text is concerned with language development.

Shayer (1991) This is an academic paper that provides a critical analysis of the cognitive development (Piagetian levels) of pupils that is needed for them to access different levels in the National Curriculum. It also plots the range of developmental levels of pupils between the ages of 7 and 16.

Smith *et al.* (1998) The general growth of children's school-based knowledge is documented in the National Curriculum structure for England but a useful alternative perspective is set out for Chicago in this report.

Reading

Aaron (1997) There are numerous texts that deal with reading, but Aaron's paper is very recent and it provides an authoritative summary of research and the remedial approaches taken for children who are having trouble with either decoding or comprehension.

Goswami and Bryant (1990) An important text that deal with the links between reading and phonological awareness.

Origins of the alphabet

Oriental Museum in Durham There is a permanent excellent exhibition of the development of writing and this outlines the origins of alphabetically based script.

Holidays

The importance of holidays on student learning is examined in some detail in **Cooper *et al.*** (1996) and a nice analysis of Dutch data is presented in **van den Bergh and Kuhlemeier** (1992). The importance of the holiday effect for tests that report age-standardised scores is discussed in **Tymms** (1998a).

Arithmetic

Thompson (1997) This text brings together a collection of writings about number development in young children and provides some interesting insights.

Bielinski and Davison (1998) A recent academic article, which looks at the more homogeneous maths scores of girls, when compared with boys.

Cultural Capital

Kelly *et al.* (1984) The assessment of Cultural Capital was put into questionnaire form by Alison Kelly as part of the Girls into Science and Technology project.

Twins and higher multiples

The book by **Cooper** (1997) gives a broad advice to the parents of twins and higher multiples and a recent report of research can be found in **Tymms and Preedy** (1998).

Attention Deficit Hyperactivity Disorder

Cooper and Ideus (1996) A teacher's guide to ADHD.

Merrell (1998) A conference paper which summarises much of the findings from the PIPS project in relation to ADHD.

Scientists and science

Accounts of scientists are always fascinating and **Gleick** (1992) provides an excellent biography of Richard Feynman. George Washington Carver's astounding story is told in **Eysenck** (1995).

Tymms (1996b) This technical report analysed the 1991 Key Stage 1 results connected to the 1995 Key Stage 2 results.

Sex differences

See references at the end of Chapter 1.

School difference

See references at the end of Chapter 4.

1. Middle schools are involved in the Performance Indicators in Middle Schools (PIMS) project and this includes Year 8.
2. This is a slight under-estimate since the pupils were not shown all possible letters. It does, however, compare girls and boys objectively.
3. What is meant by an Effect Size in this context? An Effect Size is the difference between scores expressed in Standard Deviations. In order to work out an Effect Size for school differences we choose two particular schools and work out the difference between them in Standard Deviations using the Standard Deviation of the pupils' scores. But which two schools should be chosen? The decision is based on Standard Deviations of the school averages. One school is chosen that is one school-level Standard Deviation above and another that is one school-level Standard Deviation below the average.

Notes

Chapter 4

Value-added

If we look at school league tables there is a temptation to think that the schools at the top of the table are the best schools and that the schools at the bottom are the worst. But it does not take more than a moment's thought to realise that this is a premature conclusion. A school might find itself at the top of the league table in spite of providing a poor education. Its pupils might have started at the school at a higher level in the first place or there might be other explanations. A similar kind of problem arises when we try to assess the importance of homework. The academic achievements of children who do a lot of homework might be higher than those who have done little. But sometimes we find that the pupils who have done the most homework have the lowest scores. We hope that this is not because the homework has done them harm, although we should not reject that possibility out of hand. It is much more likely that the pupils who were falling behind were given more work to help compensate.

The point is that a simple judgement on the basis of an association is unjustified. Whether we are comparing the achievements of pupils who did different amounts of homework or the league table positions of schools we need to be cautious. In order to make fair comparisons we need to compare like with like. If we can do this then we will be able to start to say something meaningful about different schools and the impact of homework on learning.

The only truly fair way to compare like with like is to send identical groups of pupils to different schools, or to give identical groups of pupils different amounts of homework. Now, getting identical groups of pupils sounds pretty difficult, and it would not be possible to organise the whole country to have identical groups of pupils starting in every school every year. However, it is possible to give homework, in varying amounts, to almost identical groups of pupils. The way to do this involves randomisation and more is said about this in the final chapter. The technique will not, however, provide a steady stream of information for schools about how their pupils are progressing. To do that we must look for other techniques which are designed as proxies for random assignment and which still seek to compare like with like. These techniques are never as definitive as experiments but they can provide useful information. The main approach leads to Value-added scores that are becoming more and more important in education.

The term Value-added is very unfortunate. It has two quite different meanings and this causes considerable difficulties that lead to confusion. There is the common sense meaning of the term, which is to add value to something. Using this interpretation we could say that we add value to pupils in our schools by teaching them to read. Pupils arrive in our schools unable to read (only about 1 per cent[1] of pupils can read when starting in reception). Then within three years they can all read (true of 94 per cent[2] by Year 2). So our schools have 'added value' to the pupils.

However, this simple interpretation of Value-added, as progress, is not the way that it is being used in education today. The modern educational use of the term refers to the *relative* progress of pupils, or how well pupils read compared to other pupils with similar starting points. This is the meaning of the term used by school effectiveness researchers, QCA and the *Times Educational Supplement* (depending on who is writing the article). But although the term is regrettable the concept behind it is very valuable and it will be illustrated with data from pupils who started school in 1994 and took their end of Key Stage 1 assessments in 1997. The explanation that follows will be graphical but for those who prefer words it is hoped that the text is sufficiently clear for the concept to be understood.

Pupils are assessed with the PIPS baseline assessment when they first start school. The average standardised score is 50 and two thirds of pupils have scores between 40 and 60. Only a very small proportion have scores below 30 or above 70.

When the pupils reach Year 2 they are given levels in the Key Stage 1 statutory assessments. The concept of Value-added involves linking the baseline assessment to the Key Stage levels and in the example that follows the average Key Stage 1 level has been used. It is calculated from the reading, writing, spelling and maths levels. Plotting a graph makes the link between the baseline results and the levels visible. An example appears in Figure 4.1. The diagram shows 350 pupils who took their end of Key Stage 1 assessments in 1997. Every little square represents a pupil. John, for example, scored 30 on the baseline assessment and got a Level 1 on average at Key Stage 1. Jane got 67 on the baseline assessment and a Level 3 at Key Stage 1.

The diagram tells us that pupils who got high scores in the baseline assessment *tended* to get high Key Stage 1 levels and vice versa. The tendency is not so clear-cut as to make the pupils' future success predictable in a definite way. We can only have a general idea about how well they are going to do. If we could predict their Key Stage 1 levels with precision all of the little squares on the scattergram would

4.1 *The meaning of Value-added*

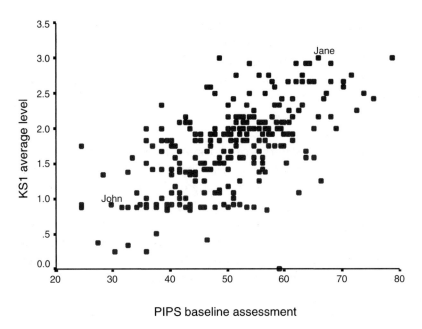

Figure 4.1   Scattergram linking baseline to Key Stage 1

be on a straight line. The correlation between the two measures would be perfect. The tendency for dots to run from the bottom left to the top right is clear and the correlation is 0.6. If the same exercise is carried out from GCSE to A level the correlation is similar. In fact much of school effectiveness is based on this kind of relationship and the correlations rarely go above 0.7.

Having established a reasonable connection between the baseline assessment and Key Stage 1 average levels the next stage is to summarise the relationship. Adding a line to the scattergram can do this. This line is sometimes called the line of best fit and it is shown in

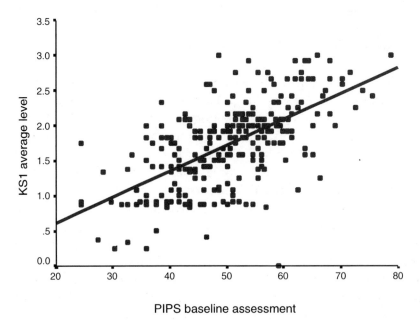

Figure 4.2   Scattergram with line of best fit

Figure 4.2. It shows the Key Stage level that would be expected for a pupil who started with a particular baseline assessment score. For example, if a pupil had a baseline score of 55 then we would predict a Level 2 on average in Year 2. We do this by reading figures off from the line of best fit.

The line, and the predictions that we can make from it, put us in a very powerful position because we can now compare like with like. We can compare pupils who had the same baseline score with one another. Consider a pupil who started school with a baseline score of 70. Pupils who start with 70 tend to finish up with a level 2.5. So, if Sunil starts with 70 and finishes with a level 3 he has done better than expected by half a level. We could also say that, compared with other pupils with the same starting point, he has done better by half a level. The amount that he has done 'better than expected' is called Value-added and it corresponds to the vertical distance from the line of best fit. Some pupils will have positive Value-added scores and some will have negative. Most pupils will be close to the line and so their Value-added scores will be small. If they are exactly on the line their Value-added is zero.

With the pupils above the line just balancing those below the line the average Value-added score will always be zero. This will allow some future Secretary of State for Education to announce to the waiting press that the average Value-added for our primary schools is zero! This will worry the public as much as knowing that half our pupils are below average; yet another reason to regret the term 'Value-added'.

In statistics Value-added has traditionally been called the residual and it would be better if we could turn the clock back and continue to use that term. But reality must prevail and the terms residual and Value-added will be used interchangeably for the rest of this book.

Readers who are meeting with this concept for the first time, and those who have had some time to think about it, will doubtless have a number of questions to ask at this stage. In an attempt to anticipate these queries several of the questions that have been raised in the past are posed below. The whole procedure is known by the glorious title of 'Ordinary Least Squares Regression Analysis' and many texts, research papers and computer programs are devoted to it. Anyone wanting to probe more deeply will find references later in this book.

4.2.1 Is the position of the line important?

The position of the line is crucial. It summarises all of the information carried in the pupils' assessments and it is used to make decisions. If the line is to be used in comparing schools it should be based on high quality representative data. If it is being used within a school to look at individual pupils' results then the exact position of the line is not quite so important, but care should be taken none the less.

4.2 Questions about the Value-added approach

4.2.2 How do you decide where to draw the line?

The most accurate way to draw the line and the one that is used by researchers is to use a computer program. But, with a little practice it is possible to draw quite a respectable line through the points on a scattergram. To do this a few hints might be helpful. First, it is useful to draw the line with a clear plastic ruler so that you can see the marks on the scattergram as you try moving the ruler around to check out how the line might look in different places. The line of best fit will have the points balanced equally above and below it.

Next, it is useful to know that the line goes through the grand mean. That is to say it goes through a point which corresponds to the average for each of the measures. This is, incidentally, the centre of gravity of the points on the scattergram. Finally, you might have noticed that the points on the scattergram seem to form the shape of an ellipse. The line should go through the two vertical tangents to the ellipse. This is shown in Figure 4.3 where the dot represents the grand mean.

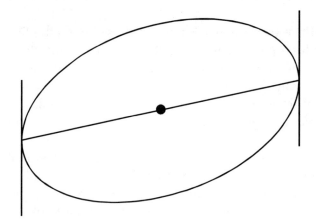

Figure 4.3   Drawing the line of best fit

4.2.3 Does the line have to be straight?

No, the line does not have to be straight and very often a slight curve is detectable. However, for most educational cognitive data, where the assessments have been well measured, a straight line is an excellent approximation. Certainly the conclusions reached when based on a curve or a straight line are nearly always the same.

4.2.4 What if some able pupils cannot show their achievement levels?

This is something to think about carefully. A good assessment is able to recognise the fact that some of our pupils are very able indeed. But many assessments have a 'ceiling' on them and some have a 'floor'. At the end of Key Stage 1, for example, a proportion of pupils is achieving at a higher standard than Level 3 would suggest. This is not recognised in the reported levels. If they had made massive progress since the baseline assessment this would not show up in either the statutory assessment or the Value-added score. This is a difficulty that we must recognise. Schools that teach such high achievers might well want to use assessments, such as PIPS, that record higher levels of achievement than the statutory assessments.

Despite this we should also note that it is not a major problem in the Value-added approach used to compare schools since the very exceptional pupils are rare even for high scoring schools. We always need to be aware of the danger but in systems where checks have been made this has not been found to be a major issue.

4.2.5 Wouldn't it be best to get a low score to begin with?

Yes indeed, a lower baseline score would ensure a higher residual and this indicates a way forward for the cynical and a danger in the whole procedure. If a school deliberately gave low baseline scores to its pupils it would get inflated Value-added scores later. If a school manipulated its Key Stage 1 levels so that they were low then it could improve its Year 6 Value-added results. One might think that professionals would not do such a thing and that might well be the case. However, if the Value-added scores become 'high stakes', in the sense that teachers' salaries or jobs depend on the results, then professionalism might be strained too far. This opens up a whole range of questions about data and how it is used. If the information is for schools and teachers, to help them with their own responsibilities, then there should be no difficulty. If, on the other hand, the information is for outsiders then the situation changes – now the aim is to hide difficulties not to search them out.

4.2.6 Is it really fair?

We have already seen that the aim of the Value-added approach, or regression analysis as it is sometimes called, is to compare like with like. In doing so, it aims to make fair comparisons and a lot rests on this. Schools are being compared using Value-added scores and policy decisions are made on the basis of its findings.

The most honest answer to the question 'is it really fair?' is that we can never be certain. But we can make informed comments and recognise that there are degrees of fairness. It is clearly very unfair to compare schools on the basis of raw league tables and it is certainly fair to compare large groups that were created by random assignment. Value-added measures are somewhere in between these two extremes. If done well, and if based on high quality data, regression procedures provide the fairest performance indicators available. But those 'ifs' should not be ignored. If one tried to compare a school in a tough area where English is an additional language for all pupils with a school in a leafy suburb where English is a first language for all, then no amount of clever statistics would make for a fair comparison. Like would simply not be being compared with like. There are limits to the approach. As a general rule problems (misinterpretations) are most likely to appear in unusual cases and that means schools or pupils with exceptional intakes or scores.

4.2.7 What happens if there is more than one predictor?

The technique described earlier, for calculating Value-added scores (regression analysis), can be based on more than one predictor. For example, one could work out Value-added measures based on a prior achievement measure as well as a measure of home background. It would be hard to draw the scattergram, which would now be in three dimensions, but the idea behind the technique would be just the same – comparing like with like. The residuals would correspond to how much better (or worse) a pupil was doing compared to others with the same score on the earlier assessment *and* from the same home background. When more than one predictor is used the technique is known as multiple regression.

It is also possible to work out Value-added scores separately using the different predictors. Within the PIPS project we calculate Value-added scores based on prior achievement and on the basis of developed ability. This provides two measures of Value-added which are often in agreement but when they do differ they provide important diagnostic information to the teacher.

4.2.8 Does Value-added have to use prior achievement?

To be fair to schools the main predictor should be a cognitive measure and an earlier achievement measure is useful. But a slightly different Value-added measure is found if a developed ability measure is used as the predictor. Sometimes the developed ability measure is collected a year or more earlier than the outcome measure but using a concurrent measure can produce useful information. We find that Value-added measures calculated from prior achievement and concurrent developed ability measures tend to give similar results. But there can be differences and it makes sense to have both where that is possible.

4.2.9 Can Value-added be used to check standards over the years?

No. To compare standards over the years researchers need to ask representative samples of pupils the same questions year on year. Even then there will be difficulties but that is another story.

4.2.10 Where does multi-level modelling come in?

Sophisticated versions of regression analysis have been developed recently in a number of different sites around the world. These are known as multi-level models and enable some very complex analyses of data to be carried out. Fortunately, when comparing schools, the results from the multi-level analyses are invariably identical to the results from the much simpler analyses.

4.2.11 Is benchmarking the same as Value-added?

No, benchmarking is an inadequate cheap substitute for Value-added. Schools and teachers will be seriously misjudged by its use. The problem is that benchmarking depends on finding schools that are similar using features such as the percentage of its pupils receiving free school meals. But very different pupils can populate schools with the same percentage of free school meals. It is only by starting with high quality information on individual pupils that credible comparisons can be made.

4.3 Value-added in one school

If a school decided to work out its own Value-added scores it would be of limited use because its average residual would always be zero. On the other hand the process could give interesting information about individual pupils. Those with very low residuals are pupils who have made less progress than expected. In exceptional cases teachers will almost certainly know why those pupils have not progressed as expected. There may have been a long absence from school for some reason, or there may have been some family difficulty and so on. Explanations for most of the unusual scores can often be found, but occasionally there will be scores that do not fit the school's perceptions. It is then that questions need to be asked. Were the scores misleading? Was there something that the teacher missed? Was the pupil more capable than he or she had shown during the last year?

As with all information of this kind it adds an extra dimension. It allows the school and the teacher to see their pupils from a different angle. In most cases the new information will correspond well with the old but occasionally it will throw up something new and it can also highlight something that has been taken for granted for some time.

4.4 Differences between teachers and schools

School effectiveness research, which looks at differences between schools, is now more than 30 years old. It started with a massive piece of research in the United States that resulted in the Coleman report. The 1966 report is often quoted as saying 'schools do not matter'. In fact it said no such thing but it did state that: 'equalising the financial resources available to schools would reduce the inequalities by less than one per cent'. This conclusion appears to be saying that school resource levels do not matter. This is worrying since it justifies low spending on education and it was based on extensive research. Coleman and his colleagues surveyed more than 600,000 pupils, assessing their academic attainment with specially administered tests. Input measures such as socioeconomic status, gender and ethnic origin were also collected. A Value-added approach was used and the residuals were related to the resources available to each school. Little connection was found.

Many researchers challenged the findings and started their own careful studies. Rutter and other researchers carried out one of those studies in 12 London comprehensive schools. Among other things they concluded that:

> Even when comparisons between schools were restricted to children who were quite similar in family background and personal characteristics prior to secondary transfer, marked school variations remained. This meant that children were more likely to show good behaviour and good scholastic attainments if they attended some schools than if they attended others.

How is it then that well-respected researchers working in similar fields can produce such apparently contradictory findings? In the first place one must establish that there is indeed a clear difference between the findings. In particular were they actually measuring the same things when they compared schools? One crucial point here is the outcome measures of the studies. In the USA the 'achievement tests' were essentially speeded multiple-choice tests of a rather general nature – somewhat akin to ability tests – whereas within the UK the studies could focus on achievement tests which assessed what pupils and teachers have been working towards together. There was a syllabus and there were examples of past papers. Furthermore, the Coleman report *did not* say that schools do not matter but the message perceived by many was just that. It could simply be as Reynolds suggests that the zeitgeist of the time was such that the idea that schools did not make a difference found an echo in prevalent sociological theories.

One of the results of the worldwide study of school effectiveness is that we now have well refined tools for monitoring schools and we can be confident of findings that appear again and again in the literature.

Whenever Value-added scores are calculated the differences between pupils are partially 'explained'. We can see that in the Figures 4.4 and 4.5 in which the spread of residuals are set alongside the spread of scores before controls were made.

The box-and-whisker plots show a reduction in the spread of scores for pupils and for schools. In other words the process of regression analysis helps to 'explain' some of the differences between schools. The figures show this and for illustrative purposes the scale used in the two diagrams is the same.

The reduction of school differences in Value-added scores is important. The differences between schools that are seen in raw league

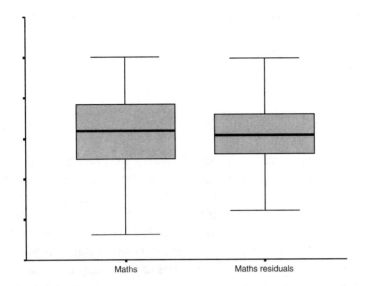

Figure 4.4   Reduction in the spread of pupils' scores

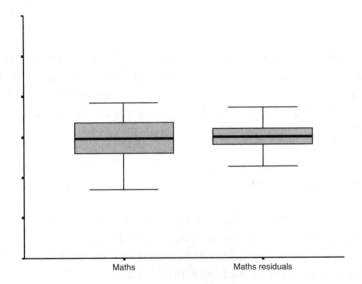

Figure 4.5   Reduction in the spread of schools' scores

tables are largely due to the differences in the pupils that go to the schools. If the Value-added process does not help to explain differences then there is a problem. In fact baseline assessments can use this as one of the markers to help validate their schemes. Occasionally schools look more different on Value-added score than they do on the raw data and this flags serious problems with the measures.

Because the Value-added approach seeks to compare like with like it can be used as a research tool. It gives much clearer answers to questions than does the simple comparison of raw data. In an earlier section we looked at how attainment varied by age, sex, home background and other variables. Now we can ask how these variables

4.5 Seeing pupil differences in context

relate to the relative progress. In other words we will compare pupils with similar starting points.

4.5.1 Age

Younger pupils tend to have lower achievement scores than older pupils. But when Value-added is calculated low scoring pupils are compared with low scoring pupils, high scores with high scores and so on. The result of this is that age is not important in Value-added calculations. This statement is not simply a theoretical position, we looked at this issue very carefully in the Value Added National Project and confirmed that it holds with data between the end of Key Stage 1 and Key Stage 2. Of course, when very large datasets are considered statistically significant differences can be found but they are small and often distract from the main features of the information.

4.5.2 Sex

The same points made about age hold for sex. We have already seen that differences between boys and girls are not very great when achievement is measured using high quality instruments. When residuals are compared the differences are smaller and their importance decreases.

4.5.3 Home background

Once we have used Value-added procedures to take into account a cognitive measure such as prior achievement, home background measures are of little importance. This statement, however, holds for pupils but does not always hold for schools. This distinction is important and needs a little clarification. If we compare the pupils' residuals then we find that pupils from affluent and deprived families tend to have very similar results. But when we find the average residuals for schools in affluent and deprived areas we find that the residuals in affluent areas tend to be higher. This is not a large effect but for schools with unusual intakes it can be important and it often appears in school effectiveness studies. It is referred to as the 'contextual effect'. Sometimes it is measured by the percentage of its pupils taking free school meals, sometimes by the average baseline score of the school or by the average socioeconomic status of the parents. But whichever way it is measured it presents a dilemma. Should we take the school's context into account after having taken individual pupil characteristics into account?

If we were presented with such a stark choice the answer is surely 'no'. If we 'control' for background features as well as prior achievement then we are saying that pupils who attained a certain academic level by the age of, say, seven are expected to make less progress in a junior school that is situated in a less affluent area. This position needs to be considered carefully. A child of seven who has attained a particular level has done so from his or her own background which has presumably had more influence over him or her during those seven years than it ever will again. If he or she has a high level of attainment despite an unpromising home background then he or she must have something special. Are we to say nationally that we expect him or her to fall away? If anything we should expect the opposite.

But our choice is not so stark. We are able to look at Value-added scores calculated with and without the school's context. If we do this and find different pictures then we will need to consider some possible explanations. Some reasons for differences follow in the bullet points below but words are not wasted on trying to argue that one of the explanations is the best. We simply do not know.

- The prior achievement measures may not be adequate. Unreliability in the measures will result in schools from tough areas being misjudged. This will show up as a contextual effect.
- Peer effects – the combined effects of all the children in the class may lift the group as a whole (or depress it).
- Recruitment of staff. It may be easier to recruit staff for some schools than others and this may ultimately show itself as a contextual effect.
- A class of successful children may lead the teacher to better teaching and all pupils might benefit.
- There may be more parental support in some areas and this, through financial or other help, may have a systematic effect on schools.
- There may be a high turnover of teachers and / or pupils in tough areas.

4.5.4 First language

The same arguments that applied to age and sex in Value-added apply to pupils whose first language is not English but with some modifications. There is a reasonable expectation that children starting school with little English will learn the new language very rapidly. These pupils might then be expected to have positive residuals – at least in the first few years at school and we have seen some slight evidence for this.

4.5.5 Twins and other multiple births

We have found little difference between the progress made by singles and by twins or triplets.

4.6 The limitations of the Value-added approach

Statistically the Value-added approach is trustworthy. The underlying processes of regression analysis have been exhaustively investigated and it is a technique that is well understood. However, the Value-added measures can only be as good as the information that is put into the calculation. The aim of regression is to compare like with like and unless there is good accurate data on which to make the comparisons all is lost. In practice the data are not perfect and it is important to acknowledge this and to be aware of just how good the data are. There are, however, some clear difficulties that can be avoided.

- When comparing the attainments of pupils in different schools using a Value-added approach the controlling variables must include cognitive data. To carry out a Value-added analysis using home background variables is not sufficient.
- The controlling variables must be based on objective data. The use of subjective data undermines the whole approach. A harsh, or lenient, approach will have a knock-on effect when it comes to calculating residuals.
- A further threat to the quality of data comes from the pressure that teachers and schools are put under. If the data become corrupted then the Value-added measures are useless.
- Value-added methods are at their weakest when they try to deal with very unusual pupils or schools. Schools with very high proportions of pupils with free school meals, or pupils whose first language is not English, need to be dealt with separately.

4.7 Summary and suggestions for further reading

In this chapter the Value-added approach to monitoring schools is explained and explored. The concept is essentially simple in that it allows like to be compared with like by controlling for important variables. However, there are many potential complexities associated with the concept. A series of frequently asked questions are answered and then a series of relationships are considered. This includes the relationship of Value-added scores to schools, the ages of pupils, sex, home background, first language and twins. Generally, Value-added measures show little connection with variables describing pupils. The most interesting differences are associated with schools and teachers.

Statistics

Readers who would like to follow the statistical aspects of Value-added are urged to look at the texts recommended at the end of Chapter 1. (The topic is referred to as 'regression' in those texts and the Value-added measures are called residuals.)

The issues surrounding Value-added

Fitz-Gibbon (1997) For those who would like to look more deeply into the issues surrounding Value-added then the best approach is probably to consult the reports from the Value Added National Project which are summarised in the Final Report. It also holds important warnings about the limitations of the whole approach and there are a series of technical reports that hold detailed investigations of many of the issues discussed. The four reports related to primary education explore many of the issues using Key Stage data as well as data derived from the PIPS project.

Multi-level modelling

Paterson (1991) For those who would like a straightforward introduction to complexities of multi-level modelling the chapter provides a good start.

Computer programs

Readers who would like to work with data at a computer will find the following three programs useful.

Excel A very widely available program that lets the researcher manipulate data in complex ways and produce good diagrams. It is not a dedicated statistics program and is therefore limited in some ways.

Minitab A nice statistics package which is easy to learn. It was designed to teach statistics and retains much of that user friendliness. It can produce excellent diagrams.

SPSS (Statistics Package for the Social Sciences) is the workhorse of the social sciences. There is little that SPSS cannot do.

School differences and school effectiveness

There are numerous texts on school effectiveness but the following four are of considerable interest.

Coleman *et al.* (1966) This is the report that started the whole school effectiveness movement in the first place.

Rutter *et al.* (1979) A classic text which stimulated much research around the world. In many ways it looks dated in the numbers of schools involved and in the statistics employed but it is well worth reading.

Teddlie and Stringfield (1993) An excellent summary of an important 10-year study.

Teddlie and Reynolds (1999) Destined to become the bible of school effectiveness study for years to come.

The contextual effect

The contextual effect referred to is discussed further in **Willms** (1992) when he refers to Type A and Type B school effects. It is also considered by **Tymms** (1992) in relation to the varying impact of different types of A level provision.

Notes

1. Taken from the PIPS baseline assessment data.
2. This is the proportion of pupils that Year 2 teachers do not identify as 'non-readers' during Year 2 assessments

Chapter 5

Attitudes

We saw, at the start of the book, how a measure called Attitude to School was constructed. It involved asking Year 6 pupils to respond to a series of statements such as 'I like school'. Any one of the statements generates responses that give a measure of attitude to school but each one is limited. They are limited by the number of possible responses that is offered and by the questions themselves.

In trying to measure an attitude the aim is to gauge the feelings of an individual as accurately as possible. We might think in terms of asking pupils to mark their feeling on a finely differentiated scale. Maybe a 10-point scale or a 30-point scale would be a good idea. Our experience suggests that a three-point scale up to the age of seven is as finely differentiated as makes practical sense. A five-point scale for older primary children works well. We also find that the older children manage a word-based scale but diagrams are better with younger children. With seven-year-olds, for example, we ask them to respond by putting a ring round the most suitable face after the teacher has read out a statement:

I like school

Because the aim is to gauge feelings we try to allow pupils the option of being neutral. If they do not feel decisive we do not want to force an idea out of them. There is always a 'not sure' or neutral option available. In fact the vast majority of primary children's responses tend to be positive and this is even more true of seven-year-olds than it is of 11-year-olds.

Asking a lot of questions and then finding the average response circumvents the problem of the number of possible responses limiting the measure. In Year 2 we ask seven questions each of which have three options when looking at Attitude to School. The scale then has 15 points on it giving a finely differentiated measure.

The second issue, the precise wording of the question limiting the measure, is also circumvented. Each question may not quite represent what it is that we want to ask. Each may be too particular or hold an idiosyncratic meaning for some respondents. By using many questions these bumps are ironed out giving us more confidence in the final measure.

Having created a suitable scale we still need assurance that the scale is reliable and that it is picking up the kind of information that it was designed to pick up. These questions of reliability and validity are important and whilst we are confident that the PIPS project scales have high internal consistency and good construct validity we need to explore some of the other issues more thoroughly in the future.

We do not try to collect attitude information from pupils at the start of Reception but we do collect such information at the end of the year and then again in Year 2, Year 4, Year 6 and Year 8. We have more confidence in the data that we have collected on older pupils. Partly because of this much of what follows in this chapter is concerned with 11-year-olds, although it must be accepted that some pupils can respond rather oddly!

5.1 General patterns

Throughout the primary age range pupils are generally very positive about school and about the things that they are taught. The positive attitudes of pupils towards school in Year 6 has already been discussed but the positive response of primary pupils is a general finding across all ages and domains. It should be a cause for considerable celebration. In Year 2, for example, two thirds of all pupils pick the smiling face when asked to respond to the statement 'I look forward to school'. Unfortunately that generally positive attitude declines slowly as pupils get older and there is evidence to suggest that this decline continues as pupils move into their teens.

We also find systematic differences between the different areas that we ask pupils to respond to. They are generally more positive towards reading and school than they are towards mathematics. The reasons for this are not clear. Some have suggested that mathematics can generate negative feelings because pupils can very rapidly meet failure when faced with mathematical tasks. Others have suggested that it is because teachers are themselves less positive about maths. But whatever the underlying reason the finding is consistent and may well carry forward to adulthood.

But these general patterns hide the enormous variations that are seen from pupil to pupil. At all ages and in all areas there are pupils who are extremely positive and there are those that are consistently negative. In amongst this variation one expects to find patterns and the next sections look to see if there are systematic differences between various groups of pupils.

This question can be taken in two ways. One would be to ask if pupils who are positive are still positive a month or a year later. It could also be taken to ask if pupils who are positive about one aspect of schooling are also positive about other aspects. Table 5.1 helps to answer the latter question. It shows the correlations between the attitudes of pupils in Year 6 to four areas. The correlations are all positive and vary from 0.26 for the correlation between attitude to maths and attitude to reading to 0.47 for the correlation between attitude to maths and attitude to school. These correlations are modest. They give some support for the view that pupils are consistent in their attitudes but they are low enough to show that pupils are discriminating. Other researchers have found weaker relationships between attitude measures.

5.2 Are pupils consistent in their attitudes?

Table 5.1 Correlations between attitude measures in Year 6

	Attitude to maths	Attitude to reading	Attitude to science
Attitude to reading	0.26*		
Attitude to science	0.32*	0.28*	
Attitude to school	0.47*	0.43*	0.32*

* p < .01

A simple explanation of the different attitude responses of pupils might be that those who do well at something are more positive towards it. This view is not borne out in the table of correlations shown in Table 5.2. Although most of the correlations are positive they are very small. The highest is 0.18 for the correlation between reading attainment and attitude to reading. These low figures are unexpected. Other research has generally found a more positive relationship and there are some complications to consider. One theory, known as the Big-Fish-Little-Pond Effect suggests that pupils who achieve more feel better but that they also compare themselves with others. When they achieve highly but others achieve still more then that can knock their self-esteem. This means that although the pupils' attitudes will be positively correlated with achievement they will be negatively correlated with the average ability of their peers. This view has received empirical support from the work of Marsh and more detailed analyses of the PIPS data also shows the same relationships. All this implies that there is a positive although fairly weak underlying connection between attitudes and achievement, but that it is masked by other relationships.

When considering these relationships it is necessary to issue a health warning. Just as correlation does not mean causation, a lack of correlation does not mean no causation. The Big-Fish-Little-Pond Effect gives some indication of possible causes but there are others. It could be that being successful at mathematics encourages positive attitudes towards the subject but simultaneously generates boredom. Being very good at mathematics can sometimes attract keep-her-busy

5.3 Connection between attitudes and attainment

work. Similarly, less able children can feel discouraged by failure in mathematics but this can also bring teacher encouragement and special help.

Knowing a correlation can only stimulate speculation. We do not know why the correlations in the table are so low.

Table 5.2 Correlations between attitudes and attainment in Year 6

	Maths attainment	Reading attainment	Science attainment	Attainment generally
Attitude to maths	0.08*	–0.03*	0.00	0.02
Attitude to reading	0.05*	0.18*	0.10*	0.12*
Attitude to science	–0.07*	–0.05*	0.00	–0.04*
Attitude to school	0.02	0.03*	–0.02	0.01

* p<.01

5.4 Age

There is no connection of any educational significance between the age of the pupil and his or her attitude as can be seen in Table 5.3. The highest correlation is less than 0.1. (This is the correlation of attitudes with age within a single cohort. We noted earlier that over the years there is a slight decline in attitudes.)

Table 5.3 Correlations between attitudes and age in Year 6

Variable	Correlation	Effect Size
Attitude to maths	0.04*	0.1
Attitude to reading	0.00	0.0
Attitude to science	0.02*	0.0
Attitude to school	0.02*	0.0

* p < .01

5.5 Sex

Table 5.4 and Figure 5.1 show some interesting and complex patterns in relation to sex. On average girls are more positive than boys towards reading. The Effect Size of 0.3 shows that this is of modest importance in the classroom but as with the Attitude to School data, which was discussed in an earlier chapter, the spread of scores is important here. The girls are more homogeneous than the boys. This

Table 5.4 Attitudes in Year 6 and sex

Variable	Effect Size (in favour of girls)	SD boys	SD girls
Attitude to maths	0.0	0.79	0.74*
Attitude to reading	0.3*	0.89	0.77*
Attitude to science	–0.2*	0.70	0.70
Attitude to school	0.4*	0.78	0.66*

* p<.01

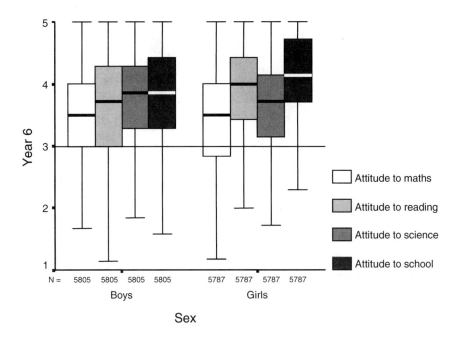

Figure 5.1   Attitudes and sex

is shown in a long tail of negative attitudes towards reading among males. The cluster of pupils who are negative towards reading (didn't like it, didn't look forward to it, and did not enjoy it) are almost exclusively boys.

Girls' and boys' attitude towards maths and science are very similar, as Table 5.4 shows.

5.6 Home background

Children from more educationally oriented homes are generally more positive towards school as well as towards reading, maths and science. The relationships is weakest for maths and science with correlations of 0.15 but the relationship is educationally relevant for attitude to reading. Children from more supportive homes (see Table 5.5) are considerably more positive.

Table 5.5   Correlations between attitudes and Cultural Capital

Variable	Correlation	Effect Size
Attitude to maths	0.15*	0.3
Attitude to reading	0.32*	0.7
Attitude to science	0.15*	0.3
Attitude to school	0.20*	0.4

* $p < .01$

The box-and-whisker plots (Figure 5.2) show that the most negative pupils came from the homes with the lowest Cultural Capital scores.

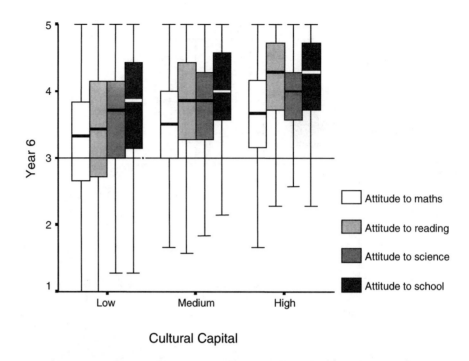

Figure 5.2   Attitudes and Cultural Capital

5.7 Developed ability

The relationship between attitudes and developed ability is slight and not of educational significance (Figure 5.3). The comments concerning the apparently weak connection between attitudes and achievement apply also to attitudes and developed ability.

Table 5.6   Correlations between attitudes and developed ability

Variable	Correlation	Effect Size
Attitude to maths	0.01	0.0
Attitude to reading	0.04*	0.1
Attitude to science	−0.03*	−0.1
Attitude to school	−0.04*	−0.1

* p<.01

5.8 First language

Children whose first language is not English are slightly more positive towards school and towards the subjects taught in school (Table 5.7). The differences are not great and the Effect Size was 0.3 or less. The box-and-whisker plots (Figure 5.4) show that the most negative pupils tended not to come from homes where English was an additional language.

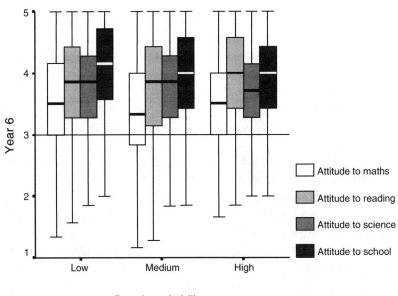

Figure 5.3   Attitudes and ability

Table 5.7   Attitudes in Year 6 and English as an additional language

Variable	Effect Size (in favour of English first)	SD English first	SD English additional language
Attitude to maths	–0.3*	0.76	0.76
Attitude to reading	–0.1*	0.85	0.79*
Attitude to science	–0.2*	0.70	0.71
Attitude to school	–0.2*	0.73	0.74

* $p < .01$

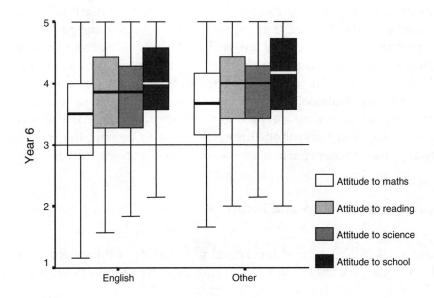

Figure 5.4   Attitudes and first language

5.9 Schools

So far this chapter has been fairly negative in its findings. There seems to be little connection between the attitudes of pupils and a whole series of variables. There are some positive relationships but they are all weak. In Table 5.8 the importance of school can be seen. The school attended appears to be more important than any of the other variables considered so far. The Effect Sizes are all around 0.7, which is certainly not to be ignored, and there are two further points to take into account.

The first is that although the results are reported for schools it is most probably the teacher that is of most significance. We do not have detailed information about which teacher took which pupil for which part of the curriculum but the data that we do have suggests that the teacher is of the greatest importance.

The second point is that the Effect Sizes estimate the general differences between schools. At the extremes the effects are much greater. In some schools the pupils are really quite negative to some aspects of school and in others they are extremely positive.

Table 5.8   Attitudes in Year 6 and school

Variable	Effect Size
Attitude to maths	0.7[*]
Attitude to reading	0.6[*]
Attitude to science	0.7[*]
Attitude to school	0.8[*]

[*] p < .01

5.10 Summary and suggestions for further reading

The attitudes of pupils are often side-stepped in school effectiveness work but it is important that the issue is not ignored and this chapter looks first at general patterns of pupils' attitudes in primary schools. This includes the finding that primary school pupils are generally very positive about school and the work that they do. The chapter then turns to differences by age, sex, home background, developed ability and first language. The connections are all fairly weak but there are theoretical explanations which suggest that the underlying connections with achievement are probably higher than the correlations suggest. The most important differences seem to be with the school attended, and teachers particularly seem to have a strong influence.

Background, theories and findings

Marsh *et al.* (1988) A good theoretical perspective of the meaning of self-esteem and of the evidence surrounding can be found in this article. They propose a hierarchical structure.

Epstein and McPartland (1976) A clear account of the measurement of the Quality of School Life and the changes that can be seen over the whole of the compulsory school age as well as differences between various groups of pupils is given in this paper. It is also possible to purchase the questionnaire described in the paper.

Marsh (1991) The Big-Fish-Little-Pond Effect concept is discussed in this paper.

Tymms (1998b). The paper by Marsh concerns secondary pupils and this one by Tymms builds on Marsh's work and is related to the attitudes of seven-year-olds in primary schools.

Tymms (1997a) This is an academic paper which looks at the attitudes of pupils towards science at the end of primary schools and how it relates to a number of other variables.

Chapter 6

How to live in a fog

We live in a complex and complicated world in which the impact of our actions is rarely certain. With the best will in the world when we aim to do something we are sometimes confronted with unexpected consequences. A rather intriguing example comes from the 1960s in the United States at the time when Martin Luther-King was involved in the march on Washington and there was growing pressure to outlaw discrimination. At that time a human rights bill was passing through Congress. It aimed to outlaw discrimination on the basis of race or creed. The right wing, looking to scupper the bill, decided to introduce into it the word 'sex'. Their purpose was to ensure that the bill would not get through because, they reasoned, nobody could possibly want to pass a bill to ensure that people would be treated the same whether they were male or female. The whole thing backfired and not only did the bill go through in the United States but similar laws were passed in many other countries. We now have legally enshrined rights which can enforce the equal treatment of males and females.

This amazing reversal can be paralleled within education, an example being the attempt to get more work out of teachers when the Conservative government laid down exactly how many hours they should work. Many were already working more hours than the number that was laid down. When teachers saw what they were *required* to do they simply refused to do the extra work for which they were clearly not being recognised or remunerated. Out-of-hours activities such as sporting events suffered and it has been suggested that this has resulted in our recent failures as a sporting nation!

At a more localised level many teachers have found that trying to achieve a particular aim in the classroom can have the opposite effect. There are also head teachers who have tried to introduce a new policy within the school that has backfired. In education, as in life, it is diffi-cult to be specific and precise about the future. It could be that the attempt to improve education by introducing OFSTED and the public humiliation of schools actually does harm. It might have decreased recruitment into education or even persuaded good teachers to leave the profession and it might have reduced creativity in the classroom. It is difficult to pin these things down, but we must accept the possibility that our attempts to push things in one direction can pull them in the opposite.

While precise prediction is impossible in human affairs and unexpected reversals do happen, a much more realistic aim, predicting what is likely to happen, is easier, at least in the short term. We can enhance our predictions by having good information about the present. We have already seen in this book just how well we can predict the future academic progress of individual pupils. Good measures let us have some idea about how well they are going to do. For groups, the predictions can be quite accurate although we must be much more circumspect about individuals. This unpredictability is not to be viewed as a bad thing. It is simply the way the world is and part of the rich tapestry of life. We would not want it to be otherwise, but it has important implications for the way that we try to change things and move forward.

The recent advances in theories to do with Chaos and Complexity fit well with this view of the world. A small, imperceptible change at one time can have massive impact later. The hackneyed idea of a butterfly's flap of the wing producing a tornado that can wreak havoc is based on careful calculations. The work of the theoretician, Lorenz, was based on three simple equations. He was able to show that the world's weather is unpredictable more than a few days ahead with any degree of accuracy. It is possible to know the seasons that are coming and the general features of those seasons, but it is impossible to have detailed forecasts of where and when it is going to rain and what the temperature will be. In other words, in something as tight and controlled as the physical world, even in a simplified mathematical model, the future is known only within certain broad bands. In the human educational world it is very much more difficult to know in advance the impact of introducing a national curriculum, compulsory assessment or a name and shame scheme. Who can know what will happen if we advise schools on the amount of homework they should give, or if we train head teachers to a prescribed formula or make any other of the recent national innovations in education? How will the initiatives interact with one another? Will the numeracy hour work in tandem with the literacy hour? What impact will the changes have on teachers' feelings of empowerment? What will the impact be on pupils? How will parents react? The questions are endless and the answers unknown.

Some readers might be wondering if it really is true that the future is as unpredictable as has been made out and a little explanation of the origin of the uncertainty might help. One reason is that the world is very complicated. People are influenced by events in their private lives, their own physical wellbeing, colleagues at work, line managers, the news and their own experiences to mention a few. This complexity would make it hard to estimate the impact of policies but there is a deeper problem. The main cause of unpredictability is not so much the complexity as the feedback loops that operate in human affairs. When a policy is implemented it has an initial impact, but then there are knock-on effects. People discuss what is happening, journalists write about it, unions debate it and separately or collectively these reactions influence the impact of the policy. The reactions in turn create their own reactions, which might or might not cause changes in the policies and so on. The situation becomes so involved that it becomes impossible to be sure how things will turn out. This is particularly problematic when we are dealing with intelligent human beings who are thinking complex thoughts about the motivations and actions of others and have, or start to have, their own agendas.

Consider punishment. Harsh punishment can result in better discipline but repeated harsh punishment might result in a riot, or it might not. A single action can trigger other actions, which multiply, as when a disturbed pebble falls onto a rock that knocks a boulder to create a landslide. This kind of mechanism probably underlies the development of rumours, the creation of movie stars and many of the 'stories' that hit newspaper headlines. More often our actions have little consequence and the effects die out rapidly. The point to emphasise is that we often cannot know which action will cause a landslide and which will cause nothing. We can, however, say that certain situations are more susceptible to landslides and even, on occasions, put probabilities on their occurrence following certain actions.

Well before the recent advances in Chaos and Complexity, Herbert Simon wrote very clearly about predictability. He noted that social phenomena are similar to the weather in the extent to which each can be forecast but he also noted that prediction works in situations of regularity or where a successful theoretical perspective guides the forecaster. More will be said of this in the next chapter in which simulations are discussed but he added another prerequisite of prediction and that is having reliable data.

6.1 Depoliticising education

Politicians often have fairly good information available to them and can have a reasonable idea about the likely impact on the public mood, in the short term, of their actions. Indeed it could be argued that the more successful politicians have had better information available to them than their rivals and that those who are unable to access or use good data are doomed. Political parties have learnt the value of surveys and focus groups. Within the more restricted world of education, researchers also have some idea about the impact of educational policies on pupils at least in the short term. But the long term is much harder and very much more important. Unfortunately our politicians have become increasingly hands-on in their approach to education and feel the need to make a mark during their period of office. It is a case of 'short-term (politician's) gain, long-term pain'.

Of course it is important to run education democratically, but that does not mean political involvement in the detailed running of schools while looking over one's shoulder for the next round of applause or vote. Education must be depoliticised, but it is not easy to see how the everyday involvement of politicians in education can be wrestled from them. From their perspective it would seem suicidal to step back from the limelight. The situation has, however, become serious. Educational policy-making must be divorced from the seemingly daily needs of politicians to announce initiatives and denounce teachers, schools and teaching. The tension that has developed between short-term political needs and the future of children is creating damage. Callaghan's Ruskin speech started a landslide that now needs to be stopped.

6.2 Monitoring systems

Operating in this ever changing unpredictable world is similar to moving through a thick and swirling fog while our 'leaders' profess to know where they are and to see the way forward clearly. In those mists of ignorance tinged with arrogance, our strategy must involve getting good information about where we are and what is happening. This is something that must be continually updated because the fog will never completely clear – we will never be sure about the way things are going to evolve. Collecting information must be an ongoing strategy. Where we cannot be sure about the way forward we must continually probe and prod to explore our changing surroundings and know a little of the way ahead. This can give us better clues about how to act in our own best interest. An informed teacher can make reasonable predictions about the attainments of his or her pupils at the end of the year and a civil servant can have a good idea about recruitment over the next six months. Information is needed about all parts of the system and that means comprehensive monitoring structures. They should help us to make decisions and give advance warning when things start to go awry. This involves being able to say 'well hang on, we have got a problem here, let us do something about it now'. This picking up information and doing something about it straight away is an important guide to action and policy and a prerequisite for changing things effectively.

But although monitoring will help we must not fall into the trap of ignoring the possible negative consequences. Monitoring systems themselves have dangers. If teachers must provide information about pupils and they know that the information might be used to 'manage' teachers then we need to worry. One of the possible impacts of such a system is to undermine the quality of the information coming out. W. Edwards Deming said, 'Where there is fear we get the wrong figures'.

When looking at ways in which education can be monitored we need to distinguish two types of system. There are professional monitoring systems (PMS) and official accountability systems (OAS). In the professional monitoring system the data are picked up and used by the workers themsleves. Examples include ALIS and PIPS. In an OAS data are collected in order to hold individuals and structures to account. Examples include league tables and OFSTED inspections.

In a PMS the information is there for the professionals within the system. It may be available to some outsiders but it is possible for a teacher, or a school, or an authority to examine their problems without exposing them to the outside world. In an OAS involving league tables, reports to the business community, the press and so on, the information is not for those working within the system but for the outside world. It is designed to provide others with information so that the schools and teachers can be held to account through market forces, public pressure and statutory arrangements.

The status of the information in the two systems is very different. Professionals within a PMS will want to use the information to find problems but within an OAS the motivation will be to hide them. This inevitably leads to tension between the accountability systems and monitoring structures and we need to be careful about those conflicts. Systems need to be in place where people are able to look at data without the fear of losing their jobs. They must be able to search for problems and deal with them without the scrutiny of the outside world.

This does not mean no accountability and no OAS, but it does mean that there needs to be some restriction on the availability of information. Some of the information must be confidential to the teacher, some to the school and some to the LEA. We already have high quality monitoring systems running smoothly within England at the moment and they need to be treated with care.

The systems will evolve in response to pressures and ideas and as they do so we need to worry about the quality of the data within them. Where there is pressure on individuals, or where there is money tied to the data, there are likely to be difficulties. This means, for example, that OAS cannot reliably be used to track standards over time. There are other reasons why it is problematic to use statutory assessments to track standards. Because they are high-stakes assessments the security around their use must be high and so new tests must be created each year. Unfortunately, comparing the standards of cohorts on the basis of different assessments is a less than perfect activity. Professional judgements must be called on and while a fairly good job can be made of it from one year to the next we can expect a steady drift in standards over time. It follows that we will have a problem in 2002 when the national targets are called to account. If we reach them we will not know if that is because the pupils have achieved higher standards or if the system has been manipulated in some way. As a nation England is unable to monitor standards over time satisfactorily. To do so we require small representative samples of pupils to be assessed on the same tests year on year. The tests need to be very carefully devised since we can expect changes to the National Curriculum in the future. A small unit should be set up to carry out the task. The benefits of such independent high quality relatively inexpensive data being produced on a regular basis would be enormous.

Nevertheless, with the monitoring structures that are already in place we are in a much stronger position when it comes to changing things. There is now extensive information about education available on a regular basis and this means that the introduction of new policies can be linked to the monitoring systems.

New ideas and pressures are arising continually and it is the resulting successful innovations that can help to improve education. But it is quite wrong to change things on a national basis without good evidence that the new ways are, or can be, effective. Things should change on a small scale to see if they work in a local context first. This should be done in a situation where failure can be tolerated and experimentation encouraged. Only then should the new way be evaluated formally on a wider basis, employing trials using the evidence- based approach outlined in the next chapter. No advice should be given to schools before tight field-based evaluations have shown positive benefits. Even then the innovation should be tracked with long- term follow-up evaluations. These apparently quite reasonable suggestions have simply never operated within England. But things need to change. The future of our children is too important to continue as at present.

We have a linked problem with the monolithic National Curriculum and assessment system in our country. If we want, for example, to make a change to the assessment system for 11-year-olds at the end of Key Stage 2 we have to do it for the whole country. We cannot try out something new, get it right and after it has been shown to work let other people try it. The monolithic nature of the system is preventing innovation. The advantages of diversity and innovation have been largely lost from English education although the decision not to go for a single national baseline but to accredit different baseline assessments has shown the possibilities.

We have then three clear ways forward. First, education needs to be depoliticised. General principles and structures need to be set up by parliament but thereafter committed lifelong professionals should run the system while being accountable to parliament. Second, we need monitoring structures. Schools should be required to be able to show that they are monitoring their own provision and this probably means involvement with a PMS. There also needs to be broader national monitoring and a new small independent unit is needed to track standards over time. The third point is that we need structures within which people are free to innovate. We need diversity and the capacity to make alterations without fear. That is very different from the situation within which we are working at the moment.

We live in a fog but despite this, and the need for monitoring systems, there are things that we know about education because of some very valuable educational research. There is also much that we don't know and these issues are taken up in the next chapter.

6.3 Introducing new policies

6.4 *Summary and suggestions for further reading*

In this chapter the educational problems associated with the extreme complexity of the world within which we live are outlined. These include the difficulty of never being sure about the impact of policies. Advances in the fields of chaos and complexity help to understand this uncertainty. As a result it is argued that we need to have high quality monitoring systems in place, this being one of the crucial ways in which we can cope with a complex situation. Two types of monitoring systems are identified, Official Accountability Systems and Professional Monitoring Systems. These are characterised and discussed in relation to the way that they operate.

The increasing political involvement of politicians in the day-to-day running of education is identified as a major problem. There needs to be change which includes greater freedom to innovate and tighter evaluations before policies are introduced.

Chaos and Complexity

There are many accessible texts that deal with the ideas of Chaos and Complexity and three of the best are:

Gleick (1988) A splendidly written and exciting introduction to the ideas of Chaos.

Lewin (1993) and **Waldrop** (1993) Two books that provide similar and very readable accounts of Complexity. They take the ideas behind the study of scientific Chaos further and look at the implications offered by Complexity and the emergence of new structures.

Pritchard (1992) This practical programming guide has a chapter devoted to the Lorenz equations that deal with weather prediction.

Working in complex systems

Deming (1986) Deming is the originator of Total Quality Management. His book provides an insight into his deep understanding of organisations and how they can be run. This is the work of a guru but it is unusual in that his approach is founded on empiricism and high quality data.

Simon (1988) Although Simon wrote this book before many of the recent advances his clear thinking makes it a very worthwhile text. He is one of those writers whose work stands the test of time.

Glass (1979) A penetrating article from many years ago which calls for monitoring structures.

Tymms (1998c) The distinction that can be made between Professional Monitoring Systems and Official Accountability Systems is discussed in this chapter.

Fitz-Gibbon (1996a, 1996b and 1997) These three texts provide an excellent overview of monitoring and the rationale behind it.

Chapter 7

What we do and do not know and how we can find things out

Educational research has been an active discipline for about a century and much progress has been made especially in the methodological field. The progress has, however, been disappointingly slow at times and we saw earlier that there are probably limits to what it is possible to know. Some educational research consciously restricts itself to particular situations and is not designed for generalisation, but there are some careful pieces of work with important findings that have been reproduced often enough to give us a degree of faith that the findings are widely applicable. There are other vital areas where much work has yet to be done. This chapter first describes one important area of very successful educational research. It then goes on to outline some fields where we need to know more and finishes with a description of how we can find things out in a secure fashion and use this information in an intelligent way. The chosen example of things that have been found out relates to intervention in the early years.

7.1.1 Intervention in the early years

If a young child is being raised in very tough circumstances, in the inner city where the father is not around and the mother has low developed ability and no job, then there is good evidence to indicate that the child will benefit from early educational input. Perhaps the best known of the first intervention studies to be rigorously evaluated was the Perry Preschool Project which first ran during the 1960s in the United States and later became known as High/Scope. This programme was cognitively oriented. It was based on the work of Piaget and involved taking his theoretical ideas and translating them into practical activities for the children. The programme was intensive. Starting at the age of three the children attended five days a week for two years, excluding school holidays, and there were also home visits.

In order to be sure about the effectiveness of the programme mothers and children were first recruited and then a random sample

7.1 Clear findings from educational research

of children actually became involved in the project. It was possible to compare the children who took part in the intervention with the controls who did not. The results from comparisons in long-term follow-ups from the Perry Preschool Project, and 11 other early years interventions from the United States in the 1960s, were that children who had been involved were:

- less likely to be kept back a year at school;
- less likely to be put into a special education class;
- likely to earn more in adult life;
- more likely to own a home and a second car;
- more likely to continue with their education;
- less likely to be arrested.

These findings are powerful evidence for the importance of early education and it is also worth noting that for every dollar spent on the early intervention, six dollars were saved later on. Further follow-up studies of many similar interventions have shown Effect Sizes ranging from 0.2 to 1.0 and higher on cognitive and social development measures.

This work on early intervention has a number of key characteristics that make it of particular interest for those who look to research for improving educational provision. The first is that much work carried out has been methodologically sound. More will be said about this later but a key feature is the randomised controlled trial. Secondly the long-term follow-ups are crucial. To know that our educational efforts can have an impact years later is most important and it is even possible that early interventions can have an impact on the yet unborn next generation. The results from such two-generation studies are awaited with anticipation. The third important feature is that there have been many studies. This has been crucial because not all interventions in the early years have had positive results. What researchers can now do is to look at the different types of intervention and see what it was that marked out the successful ones. It then becomes possible to identify those areas where our knowledge is less strong and to progressively focus our attention to develop a really clear basis for action. This is not the place to consider these findings but simply to record the existence of a considerable body of research that has already been created and which is growing and should be informing our actions.

7.2 Uncertain findings

7.2.1 Homework

There are some areas where research has been active but the common sense view does not prevail. An example comes from homework in primary schools. It would seem obvious that giving extra homework is a good thing and that children will learn more if given extra work to do at home. But a recent large-scale survey in England has not supported this common sense view during the primary years. This seems hard to rationalise and there is a danger that we reject the research findings as being unreasonable unless we can see some possible explanation for the counter-intuitive finding.

We have all had the experience of trying to study and finding that we have reached a block. There is a need to take a break before coming back to the work. Persisting after reaching a sticking point may create difficulties later. In learning things, be it new concepts, skills or facts, a good way forward is to keep coming back to it. Distributed rather than concentrated work can produce the best results. Simply devoting more time to something can be counter-productive. There may also be a problem with sharing schoolwork at home. Many parents and children can describe less than positive encounters in the family home when the work is tackled together. Some parents have their own way of doing things, the child has half-learnt a different way, tension builds, the parent gets anxious about standards and so on.

So, there are good arguments for and against homework and in such a situation policy makers need high quality information. The question to ask is 'when do the benefits outweigh the negatives?' The answer to this cannot be found through discussion alone. There needs to be empirical investigation. So far as homework is concerned the best evidence so far is that homework does not make much difference to the overall progress of pupils but we need to know more and the issue is taken up again later.

7.3 Things we do not know

While there are some things that we are now fairly secure about, there is still much that we don't know. We don't know what age children should start school, or if the best approach would be to have children start at different ages according to their readiness. We don't know how best to teach arithmetic to children in primary school nor do we know how best to teach deaf children how to read. We cannot be sure that the move towards the integration of children with special educational needs into mainstream education will have the hoped for long-term benefits and we do not know if it is in the best interests of education to pay head teachers their present salaries.

In stating that we do not know these things it must be recognised that there are many who feel that they have the answers. Of course there has been research and we have theories, but in the final analysis the foundation of the claimed knowledge is shaky and there is still a great deal to learn.

In this state of partial knowledge it is not surprising to find that a common perspective is to distrust the pronouncements of researchers since they often appear to contradict one another or to be irrelevant. At times it seems almost as though the ideas of the researchers are as fickle as those of politicians. In fact, the world is not like that. We are advancing and knowledge is accumulating albeit slowly. Researchers publish their findings and they can appear to refute the findings of other groups. Arguments ensue and can involve disagreement about methodology, interpretation, analysis, samples and other details.

There is then discussion, rationalisation and further investigation and all the time we are gradually learning and creating a repository of information. At times the research seems to get caught in a blind alley and to be irrelevant to policy or practice. But an accumulation of knowledge does gradually build up. The kinds of statements that were made earlier about early intervention are not the results of one single finding but the cumulative knowledge from many different interventions in many different situations.

Academic argument can lead to advances and this is often generated by the difficulties which researchers face. The argument can lead to methodological as well as substantive advances. But although we have some sound knowledge it is important that we create new knowledge continuously. It is a tragedy that within England and elsewhere, policies are introduced without firm backing, without a good reading of the literature, and without clear evaluations from which we can learn. Time and time again we find that policies are introduced, supposedly found to be effective, and then transplanted into other situations across the land. We have noted, for example, that the research base for policies on homework is lacking and one wonders on what basis prescriptive advice is constructed. Other initiatives, for example, the Technical, Vocational Education Initiative, the Literacy Hour and the Numeracy Hour, have been set up with good intentions, then, before being properly evaluated, have been extended on a national basis.

The reader might be wondering how one can write that there is little evidence to show the efficacy of the Literacy Hour. Surely, considerable effort has gone into assessments at the beginning and the end and surely pupils have found considerable gains in their reading according to their age. There is some truth in this and there are reports to back it up. The evaluations have never, however, been unequivocal and have methodological problems. Let us consider some of the problems that arise in evaluating an introduction of an initiative such as the Literacy Hour or whatever else it might be.

7.4 Problems with evaluating policies

Suppose that the policy involves something that is going to work over a year or two years in schools and that it is a new way of working which is to be taken on board. We can assume that the project itself is going to be evaluated in terms of the outcomes of the pupils rather than the way it was carried out. So we are looking for evidence that the pupils actually gained something in the way they are reading, their qualifications, their motivation or their skills. Something at the end is going to be assessed to show that they are doing better now than they would have done had that policy not been introduced.

The first major problem is that the students themselves are likely to have been assessed, as part of the project, in precisely the way that the project itself is going to be evaluated. They might, for example, be asked to do spelling tests during the project and then asked to do spelling tests as part of the evaluation. The pupils might simply learn how to do the test without getting better at spelling generally. In other words evaluations need to be very careful about the way in which the outcome measures are chosen or constructed.

The second threat to the validity of the conclusions from an evaluation is that the group chosen to try out the policy might have had something special happen to them, other than the policy itself. A high profile project might, for example, have been reported in the *Times Educational Supplement*. Or the Local Authority might have split into smaller Unitary Authorities. Or the schools involved might have had more frequent OFSTED inspections or visits from the evaluator. Any of these might change the way that the schools function. It then becomes impossible to separate out the impact of the policy under study from the impact of other things that were happening around it.

It already seems as though any evaluation has at least two major hurdles to overcome but the biggest has to do with the groups that are involved. If the chosen group of pupils or schools are volunteers, or picked out for their special characteristics, then there is a serious threat to the validity of the evaluation as a basis for national policy. Perhaps the chosen group wanted to be part of the project, or they were volunteered by their Chief Education Officer, or they were selected because they were at the lower end of the achievement level or at the higher end and so on. This selection process undermines the evaluation because special groups are different from others in some particular way. There is one further particular point to worry about here. If the chosen group is extreme in some way, very low statutory test results for example, then we can expect their scores to be closer to the average when they are reassessed (after the policy) *even if there had been no initiative or policy change*. This phenomenon, known as 'regression to the mean', bedevils all research which involves unusual groups. It is a trap awaiting the researcher studying children with special educational needs or 'failing' schools or schools with high truancy rates or schools with very good OFSTED reports and so on.

7.5 How these problems can be avoided

The problems that are identified above, and several more, follow the analysis set out by Campbell and Stanley many years ago. They outlined a series of ways in which researchers can diagnose the problems associated with trying to assess the impact of interventions. The problems can largely be dealt with and a description of the way in which this can be done follows.

Let us consider the problem of homework during Key Stage 2. Most schools set homework during these four years and we know that there is little evidence to suggest that the amount of homework set is related to academic achievement but we want to be surer about this relationship. We want to know if it makes sense to recommend to schools that they set more. In order to set up a project to inform policy we could invite a random sample of, say 180 schools, from around the country. For statistical reasons we could keep the sample to schools with at least 30 in each year group. We will confine our interest here to the impact that a homework policy might have on the statutory assessment results at the end of primary education, but we would look at other outcomes and at the long-term impact of homework.

We would first survey the schools to see how much homework they set in the foundation subjects during Key Stage 2. We would then split the schools into three equal groups. Those that set a lot of homework, those that set moderate amounts and those that set little. The project would concentrate only on the 60 schools that set little homework. For a random 20 of these schools we would give no advice at all, for another 20 we would advise that they increased the amount of homework slightly, to that set by the middle third of schools. For the other 20 we would recommend that they increased homework setting dramatically, to that set by highest third. This advice would be backed by examples of 'best' practice and be officially supported by OFSTED inspections that would look for compliance with the advice.

Every year for the next four years we would look at the statutory assessment results of these schools and see if the advice has had any impact, but we would also be interested in what happened within each of the schools. What notice was taken of the advice? Did there seem to be a change of practice? What variations were there in the notice taken? What was the impact on the pupils' attitudes and behaviour? The evaluation would need to be diverse, detailed and careful but the main point to be made here is that this research design overcomes many of the problems identified earlier. Now we have a situation where we no longer have to worry about the fact that some will have practised the statutory assessment and some have not because each of the three groups within each of the homework categories are equivalent – or as equivalent as they can be. We don't have to worry about regression to the mean or the fact that one group was different from another because they were randomly assigned to these particular groups.

By working with the group that set the least homework there is the best chance that we can have an impact. The results of the research can directly inform policy and suggest new research.

This kind of research, sometimes called a randomised controlled trial, sometimes called experimentation, solves many of the problems which beset other research. Unfortunately, within Britain, the zeitgeist is such that this approach is often seen as an inappropriate thing to do. It is also thought to be unethical by some. But let us be clear about what we are doing. We don't know what works, we don't know what advice should be given on homework. Once we admit to our ignorance the importance of finding things out becomes imperative. It is unethical not to tackle our ignorance!

In fact this kind of research has been carried out very often and we are able now to look to the bringing together of many examples of research. One might worry, for example, that the results from a piece of work like this were only going to be applicable to those schools that year. It might only have internal validity and not generalise to other situations. By doing this kind of work over and over again, at different times and in different places, we can start to get a feel for the generalisability of the results. If we found the same result time and time again we would start to develop confidence in what we are saying. If on the other hand, we find that it worked in the 1990s in England but not in 2010 in America then we would have particular concerns and we might look for particular features of the context which would help us rationalise the discrepancies. That kind of analysis, which brings together many experimental results, is known as meta-analysis and is vital to our way forward. There are now many meta-analyses in a variety of areas of education and there are references at the end of this chapter that will allow the reader to explore further.

Experiments provide the most important and incisive way in which to test out ideas and the growing number of meta-analyses provide a vital source of information for anyone interested in policy issues within education.

As has been emphasised several times, the educational world is a complex world which is difficult to understand and difficult to predict. It is so complicated that we need continuously to monitor the state that we are in and must carry out careful research to gain what at times seem to be very small advances. Traditionally, this has been our only way forward together with attempts to construct theories that make sense of the complex findings of research and suggest new avenues for investigation and inform policy. But the world is too complicated for words. We think and write and talk linearly. A is followed by B and then by C. Our discourse can cope with a little more complexity by referring to other things that are happening simultaneously but even at its most sophisticated our traditional ways of arguing and describing are limited. Within a single interaction of two people a record of everything that happens within a half an hour could fill several volumes with the full account of sounds, intonations, eye and body movement, memory recalls, blood pressure changes, hormone releases and so on. The complexity is phenomenal and individuals are all operating simultaneously, independently and in reaction to one another. Making sense of it all seems to be almost impossible and were it not for the important progress made by research it would be forgivable to suggest that we can know nothing. Every incident would be unique and there could be no generalisations. This is clearly not the case and the purpose of theory is to try to make sense of the apparently disparate findings that we have, to see patterns in the chaos. But even here the complexity defeats us.

There is, however, light at the end of the tunnel. The advent of new hardware and software opens up the possibility of simulating the complex educational world within which we live. Each changing individual within each school can be represented as a simplified unit within a computer and allowed to run their lives within it. This simulated world could run on the structures and interactions that we

7.6 *Simulations*

believe underline the working of the world within which we live. This would allow us to try 'what if?' questions and so see if our assumptions produced the kinds of outcomes that we find in reality. It would be possible, for example, to set up a simulation in which the impact of preschool intervention could be modelled. Does the model produce similar results to carefully conducted research in the real world? If the model produces convincing results in a variety of circumstances then we might try policies that have yet to be introduced. What would be the likely impact of introducing performance related pay? What would happen if two hours of the time allocated to reading and mathematics per week in primary schools were switched to sport and music? This kind of simulation has yet to make a mark within education but the possibilities are there now and they are there to be seized.

7.7 Summary and suggestions for further reading

In this final chapter a success story from educational research is briefly recalled. It involves a series of interventions in early childhood together with long-term follow-ups. These studies provide us with a solid basis for policy even though much more research is still needed. It is also important because it shows the long term value of methodologically sound educational research.

Our present state of knowledge is, however, generally weak and much more research is needed to establish clear findings. For example, the amount of homework that should be given to primary children is not clear. On the other hand the appropriate methodologies for finding things out, randomised controlled trials, are clear. This approach overcomes many of the difficulties surrounding the more commonly employed evaluation strategies.

Finally the potential of simulations is described and hope is expressed that education will start to employ this exciting new technique soon.

Early years

Research into the early years is well summarised in a number of pieces of work and they include:

Lazar and Darlington (1982) This is the first study that brought together a set of long-term follow-ups from early interventions.

Sylva (1994) A review of much of the work in this area.

Ramey and Ramey (1998) Our present state of knowledge from early intervention studies is summarised in this paper which also provides a conceptual framework and identifies a number of gaps in our knowledge base.

Homework

Summaries of research on homework together with recent findings can be found in **Cooper** (1989), **Farrow** *et al.* and **Tymms and Fitz-Gibbon** (1992).

Literacy

A review of literacy related research including the Literacy Hour can be found in **Beard** (1998).

Randomised controlled trials

Campbell and Stanley (1966) There are numerous works on experimentation but this is the one most often quoted and it provides a solid theoretical basis for future work.

Boruch (1997) A recent fascinating account of randomised controlled trials carried out in many fields around the world. It also provides useful summaries of what has been learnt about carrying out this kind of work.

Simulations

Simulation studies have a growing number of publications. Interested readers might like to look at the on-line journal whose web address is **www.soc.surrey.ac.uk/JASSS** (See for example **Patrick** *et al.* (1999))

Tymms (1996a) Educational simulations are rare but an example can be found in this chapter.

References

Aaron, P.G. (1997) 'The impending demise of the discrepancy formula', *Review of Educational Research* **67**(4), 461–502.

Adey, P., Shayer, M. and Yates, C. (1991) *Better Learning: A report from the Cognitive Acceleration through Science Education (CASE) project.* Centre for Educational Studies, Kings College, University of London.

Beard, R. (1998) *National Literacy Strategy – Review of Research and other related Evidence (NLSRR).* London: DfEE Standards and Effectiveness Unit.

Bielinski, J. and Davison, M.L. (1998) 'Gender differences by item difficulty interaction in multiple-choice mathematics items', *American Educational Research Journal* **35**(3), 455–476.

Black, P. (1998) *Testing: friend or foe? Theory and practice assessment and testing.* London: Falmer Press.

Blatchford, P. and Cline, T. (1992) 'Baseline assessment for school entrants', *Research Papers in Education* **7**, 247–269.

Blatchford, P. and Cline, T. (1994) 'Baseline assessment: selecting a method of assessing children on school entry', *Education* **3**(13), 10–15.

Blatchford, P. *et al.* (1987) 'Associations between pre-school reading related skills and later reading achievement', *British Educational Research Journal* **13**(1), 15–23.

Boruch, R. (1997) *Randomised Experimentation or Planning and Evaluation: A Practical Guide.* London: Sage.

Campbell, A. (1998) 'Gender and the development of interpersonal orientation' in A. Campbell and S. Muncer (eds) *The Social Child.* Hove: Psychology Press.

Campbell, D.T. and Stanley, J.C. (1966) *Experimental and Quasi-experimental Designs for Research.* Chicago: Rand McNally.

Coleman, J.S. *et al.* (1966) *Equality and Educational Opportunity.* Washington DC: US Government Printing Office.

Cooper, C. (1997) *Twins and Multiple Births: The Essential Parenting Guide from Pregnancy to Adulthood.* Hull: Vermilion.

Cooper, H.M. (1989) 'Synthesis of research on homework', *Educational Leadership* **47**(3), 85–91.

Cooper, H. *et al.* (1996) 'The effects of summer vacation on achievement test scores: a narrative and meta-analytical review', *Review of Educational Research* **66**(3), 227–268.

Cooper, P. and Ideus, K. (1996) *Attention Deficit/Hyperactivity Disorder: A Practical Guide For Teachers.* London: David Fulton Publishers.

Deming, W.E. (1986) *Out of the Crisis: Quality Productivity and Competitive Position*. Cambridge: Cambridge University Press.

Epstein, J.L. and McPartland, J.M. (1976) 'The concept and measurement of the quality of school life', *American Educational Research Journal* **13**(1), 15–30.

Eysenck, H. (1995) *Genius: The Natural History of Creativity*. Cambridge: Cambridge University Press.

Farrow, S.J., Tymms, P.B. and Henderson, B. (1999) 'Homework attainment in primary schools', *British Educational Research Journal* **25**(4).

Fitz-Gibbon, C.T. (1996a) *Monitoring Education: Indicators, Quality and Effectiveness*. London and New York: Cassell.

Fitz-Gibbon, C.T. (1996b) 'Monitoring school effectiveness: simplicity and complexity', in J. Gray *et al.* (eds) *Merging Traditions: The Future of Research on School Effectiveness and School Improvement* (pp. 74–90). London and New York: Cassell.

Fitz-Gibbon, C.T. (1997). *The Value Added National Project: Final Report*. London: School Curriculum and Assessment Authority.

Fitz-Gibbon, C.T. and Morris, L.L. (1978) *How to Calculate Statistics*. London: Sage.

Furth, H.G. (1966) *Thinking Without Language: Psychological Implications of Deafness*. London: Collier-Macmillan Ltd.

Gardner, M.J. and Altman, D.G. (1989) *Statistics with confidence – confidence intervals and statistical guidelines*. London: British Medical Journal.

Glass, G.V. (1979) 'Policy for the unpredictable', *Educational Researcher* **8**(9), 12–14.

Gleick, J. (1988). *Chaos: Making a New Science*. London: Heinemann.

Gleick, J. (1992) *Richard Feynman and Modern Physics*. London: Little, Brown and Co.

Goswami, U. and Bryant, P. (1990) *Phonological Skills and Learning to Read*. Hove: Lawrence Erlbaum Associates.

Hedges, L.V. and Olkin, I. (1985) *Statistical Methods for Meta-analysis*. New York: Academic Press.

Hopkins, K.D., Hopkins, B.R. and Glass, G.V. (1996) *Basic Statistics for the Behavioral Sciences*. London: Allyn and Bacon.

Hunter, J.E. and Hunter, R.F. (1984) 'Validity and utility of alternative predictors of job performance', *Psychological Bulletin* **96**(1), 72–98.

Kelly, A., Whyte, J. and Smail, B. (1984) *Girls into Science and Technology: Final Report*. Manchester University: Department of Sociology.

Kimura, D. (1992) 'Sex differences in the brain', *Scientific American* September, 81–87.

Lazar, I. and Darlington, R. (1982) *Monographs of the Society for Research in Child Development: Lasting Effects of Early Education*. Chicago: University of Chicago Press.

Lewin, R. (1993) *Complexity. Life at the Edge of Chaos*. London: Dent.

Lindsay, G. and Desforges, M. (1998) *Baseline Assessment: Practice, Problems and Possibilities*. London: David Fulton Publishers.

Marsh, H.W. (1991) 'Failure of high-ability high schools to deliver academic benefits commensurate with their students' ability levels', *American Educational Research Journal* **28**(2).

Marsh, H.W., Byrne, B.M. and Shavelson, R.J. (1988) 'A multifaceted academic self-concept: Its hierarchical structure and its relation to academic achievement', *Journal of Educational Psychology* **80**, 366–380.

Merrell, C. (1998) *The prevalence of Attention Deficit Hyperactivity Disorder (ADHD) and its impact on academic achievement and progress*. Paper presented at the European Conference on Educational Research Ljubljana Sept. 1998.

Paterson, L. (1991) 'An introduction to multilevel modelling', in S.W. Raudenbush and J.D. Willms (eds), *Schools, Classrooms and Pupils: International Studies of Schooling from a Multilevel Perspective* (pp. 13–24). London: Academic Press.

Patrick, S., Dorman, P.M. and Marsh, R.L. (1999) 'Simulating correctional disturbances: the application of correctional control theory to correctional organisations via computer simulation', *Journal of Artificial Societies and Social Simulation* **2**(1).

Pinker, S. (1994) *The Language Instinct*. Harmondsworth: Penguin Books.

Ramey, C.T. and Ramey, S.L. (1998) 'Early intervention and early experience', *American Psychologist* **53**(2), 109–120.

Rutter, M. *et al.* (1979) *Fifteen Thousand Hours*. London: Open Books.

Shayer, M. (1991) 'Improving standards and the National Curriculum', *School Science Review* **72**(260): 17–24.

Shayer, M. (1996) *The Long-Term Effects of Cognitive Acceleration on Pupils' School Achievement*. London: King's College.

Simon, H.A. (1988) *The Sciences of the Artificial* (2nd edn). Cambridge Mass: The MIT Press.

Smith, J.B., Smith, B. and Bryk, A.S. (1998) *Setting the Pace: Opportunities to Learn in Chicago's Elementary Schools*. Chicago: Consortium on Chicago School Research.

Sylva, K. (1994) 'School influences on children's development', *Journal of Child Psychology and Psychiatry* **35**(1), 135–170.

Teddlie, C. and Stringfield, S. (1993) *Schools Make a Difference: Lessons Learned from a 10-Year Study of School Effects*. New York and London: Teachers College Press.

Teddlie, C. and Reynolds, D. (eds) (1999) *The International Handbook of School Effectiveness Research*. Lewes: Falmer Press.

Thompson, I. (ed.) (1997) *Teaching and Learning Early Number*. Buckingham and Philadelphia: Open University Press.

Tukey, J.W. (1977) *Exploratory Data Analysis*. London: Addison Wesley.

Tufte, E.R. (1983) *The Visual Display of Quantitative Information*. Cheshire, Conn.: Graphics Press.

Tymms, P.B. (1992) 'The relative success of post-16 institutions in England (including "Assisted Places Schools")', *British Educational Research Journal* **18**(2), 175–192.

Tymms, P.B. (1996a) 'Theories, models and simulations: school effectiveness at an impasse', in J. Gray, D. Reynolds, C. Fitz-Gibbon and D. Jesson (eds), *Merging Traditions: The Future of Research on School Effectiveness and School Improvement*. London and New York: Cassell.

Tymms, P.B. (1996b) *The Value Added National Project: Second Primary Technical Report*. London: SCAA. Ref. com/96/554.

Tymms, P.B. (1997a) 'Science in primary schools: an investigation into differences in the attainment and attitudes of pupils across schools', *Research in Science and Technological Education* **15**(2): 149–159.

Tymms, P.B. (1997b) 'Monitoring the progress of children during their first years at school', *Current Research in Early Childhood: OMEP Updates* Summer (No. 90), 1–2.

Tymms, P.B. (1998a) 'Opening a can of worms: a critical examination of age-standardised scores', *British Journal of Curriculum and Assessment* **8**(3), 21–25.

Tymms, P.B. (1998b) 'Schooling and the attitudes of 7-year-olds'. Paper presented at ECER Slovenia.

Tymms, P.B. (1998c) 'Accountability and quality assurance', in C. Richards and P. Taylor (eds) *How Shall We School our Children?* (pp. 171–181). London: Falmer Press.

Tymms, P.B. (1999) 'Baseline assessment, value-added and the prediction of reading', *Journal of Research in Reading* **22**(1), 27–36.

Tymms, P.B. and Fitz-Gibbon, C.T. (1992) 'The relationship of homework to A-level results', *Educational Research* **34**(1), 3–19.

Tymms, P.B. and Gallacher, S. (1995) 'Primary science: an exploration of differential classroom success', *Research in Science and Technology Education* **13**(2), 155–162.

Tymms, P.B. and Preedy, P. (1998) 'The attainment and progress of twins at the start of school', *Educational Research* **40**(2), 243–249.

Tymms, P.B. and Williams, D. (1996) *Baseline Assessment and Value-added: A Report to the School Curriculum and Assessment Authority*. London: The School Curriculum and Assessment Authority.

Tymms, P.B., Merrell, C. and Henderson, B. (1997) 'The first year at school: A quantitative investigation of the attainment and progress of pupils', *Educational Research and Evaluation* **3**(2), 101–118.

van den Bergh, H. and Kuhlemeier, K. (1992) 'A three level growth model for educational achievement: effects of holidays, socio-economic background and absenteeism', *Multilevel Modelling Newsletter* **4**(1), 7–9.

Velleman, P. (1998) *ActivStats*. Addison Wesley Interactive.

Waldrop, M.M. (1993). *Complexity: The Emerging Science at the Edge of Order and Chaos*. London: Viking.

Willms, J.D. (1992) *Monitoring School Performance: A Guide for Educators*. Lewes: Falmer Press.

Wolfendale, S. (1993) *Baseline Assessment: A Review of Current Practice: Issues and Strategies for Effective Implementation*. Stoke-on-Trent: Trentham Books.

Index